16.95

W9-ASL-384

C. W. Welch

RETRO RANCH

A Roundup of Classic Cowboy Cookin'

COLLECTORS PRESS

PORTLAND, OREGON

Copyright © 2005 Collectors Press, Inc.

All rights reserved. No part of this book may be reproduced or transmitted in any form by any means, electronic or mechanical, including photocopying, recording, or by any information storage and retrieval system, without written permission of the publisher except where permitted by law.

Design: Vicki Knapton
Editors: Sue Mann and Julie Steigerwaldt

Recipes in this book were modified from classic collections and from traditional favorites in the author's books *Oven and other Camp Cookin'* (Back Country Press, 1999); *More Cee Dub's Dutch Oven and other Camp Cookin'* (Back Country Press, 2000); and *Cee Dub's Ethnic & Regional Dutch Oven Cookin'* (Back Country Press, 2002).

Library of Congress Cataloging-in-Publication Data

Welch, C. W.
    Retro ranch : a roundup of classic cowboy cookin' / by C. W. Welch.--
1st American ed.
        p. cm.
    Includes index.
        ISBN 1-933112-00-X (hardcover : alk. paper)
        1. Outdoor cookery. 2. Dutch oven cookery. I. Title.
TX823.W44726 2005
641.5'78--dc22
                        2005000505

Printed in Singapore

9 8 7 6 5 4 3 2 1

For a free catalog write: Collectors Press, Inc., P.O. Box 230986, Portland, OR 97281. Toll free: 1-800-423-1848 or visit our website at: collectorspress.com.

Collectors Press books are available at special discounts for bulk purchases, premiums, and promotions. Special editions, including personalized inserts or covers, and corporate logos, can be printed in quantity for special purposes.

For further information contact: Special Sales, Collectors Press, Inc., P.O. Box 230986 Portland, OR 97281. Toll free: 1-800-423-1848.

DEDICATION

To Dwain and Sandy Riney, owners of Las Piedras Ranch in Real County, Texas, for giving me the opportunity to be their ranch cook. I especially enjoy the Texas Hill Country breezes softly rattling the old windmill above the ranch house, which is nestled in the hills on the headwaters of the Nueces River, while I'm tending a bunch of Dutch ovens heaped with mesquite coals. At these moments the pages of time truly are turned back for this author! Also, to all Dutch oven cooks — past, present, and future — for keeping alive the tradition of making folks smile and exclaim "Yum!" when the lid is pulled off a steaming Dutch oven. And most importantly, to my wife, Penny, for all she does to make my Dutch oven cookin' good enough for folks to ask for seconds!

CONTENTS

HOWDY!

(INTRODUCTION)

In the old days, cowboy cookin' depended just as much on the availability of ingredients as the skill of the cook. During the spring and fall roundups or on a trail drive to a northern railhead, the camp cook, or "cookie," as he was sometimes called, did not have the opportunity to saddle up and head for a grocery store to replenish the supplies for his chuck wagon. When cowboys and cookie headed out on a trail drive or roundup, they provisioned the chuck wagon before leaving the home ranch. Without refrigeration, nearly everything had to be dried. Some canned goods might have been used, but space and weight in the chuck wagon limited the selection. Staples consisted of dried beans and fruit, flour, coffee, sugar, salt, cookie's sourdough starter, and a few spices such as dried chilies, pepper, cinnamon, and nutmeg.

If the hands wanted fresh meat, it meant butchering a yearling beef or bagging a deer or antelope. The cookie would butcher enough meat for a couple of meals and "jerk" (add spices and dry) the rest. Jerky gave the cowboys something to munch on between meals. Cowboys took advantage of any opportunity to vary their usual diet of biscuits, beans, and beef. They picked wild fruit whenever they had the chance. A Dutch oven cobbler prepared with the wild fruit was enough to send even the toughest cowboy to his bedroll with a smile! Wild onions and other edible plants were used when available. The cuisine, if it could be called that, leaned toward the simple side.

Besides doing the cooking, the cookie had to set up and tear down the camp every day, rustle up enough firewood or buffalo chips for fuel, keep the water barrel full, and do a lot of other chores the cowboys thought beneath them. But, when the herd stayed in one place for a couple of days, the cookie usually went to great lengths to come up with an extra-special dish to break the monotony and help restore humor to the crew.

Cowboys didn't have much choice when it came to beverages served with their meals: Their choice was coffee or water. And anyone who has witnessed a wild cow-milking event at a rodeo knows that cream for coffee required more work than it was worth. It wasn't uncommon for the trail boss or the cookie to have a couple of bottles of moonshine stashed in the chuck wagon for medicinal purposes, but the cowboys were usually dry for long periods.

Some folks might find it hard to believe, but short of the trail boss, the most important person on a cattle drive was the cookie! A cook, either through lack of skill or desire, who didn't keep the hands happy at suppertime became a liability to the ranch owner or trail boss. Cowboys might not have many material goods, but they did have principles. It was not unheard of for a bunch of cowhands to threaten to quit or out-and-out quit — not for better pay, but for better grub! And on more than one occasion, only the trail boss's considerable diplomatic skills convincing the cook to do a better job kept a rangeland mutiny from occurring.

If anyone could get away with being grumpy, it was the cook — provided he was a good cook. But maybe cooks were all just a bunch of old grumps or perhaps they had an air about them, because they were relegated to doing what most considered woman's work. Regardless, serious consequences resulted when a cowboy irritated or teased the cookie. And when cow prices were lower than wages, many a cowboy ended up working just for room and board. Good food went a long way toward keeping the hands happy until the market improved.

When they weren't on a roundup or trail drive, cowboys worked out of ranch headquarters or a series of line shacks. The bigger ranches could afford to keep a cook at the ranch, but more often it was the rancher's wife or daughters who handled most of the cooking. When cowboys were sent to a line shack to punch cows or fix fences, they usually ended up cooking for themselves. Cooking duties were shared, or more often one poor cowpoke with no seniority ended up wearing the apron. Only when there wasn't a designated cookie was the average cowboy involved in cooking. The end result ranged all the way from starvation rations to sage brush gourmet!

Adaptability is a good trait regardless of one's occupation, but it was especially important for cookies. Things were usually pretty easy when they cooked at the home ranch. In addition to

8

a woodstove to make life easier, firewood and water were usually easy to come by, and often there was produce from the garden. Many ranches prided themselves on the wizardry of their grizzled old cooks. Given even those primitive conditions and the meager number of ingredients available, some ranch cooks became local legends. Even today descendants of the original homesteaders enjoy recipes handed down several generations.

Whether laboring over a bed of mesquite coals or sweating over an old wood range, those old cowboy cooks could whip up delicious meals that not only tasted good but would stick to the cowboys' ribs, allowing them to perform rigorous work throughout the day. Most ranchers were quick to figure out that happy cowboys made for happier cows and that a good cook went a long way toward keeping everyone happy.

As time passed civilization slowly encroached on the once-endl prairies and mount

Homesteaders, or "nesters," as some cowboys called them, started the changes by plowing prairie sod and stringing "bob wire" fences. Then it wasn't long before the transcontinental railroad and endless strings of telegraph poles became part of the western scenery. To those old trail drovers who'd pushed longhorn steers from Texas to the Kansas railheads, it was the end of an era.

But even today, 150 years since the heyday of the big-time cattle drives, the ranchers and cowboys of the American West continue the traditions started so long ago. To the ranch cooks, what the cowboys derided as progress slowly began to change the culinary scenery as well. The chugging steam engines that headed west to load beef for the eastern markets hauled fresh

produce, canned goods, kerosene for lamps, and a myriad of other products formerly unavailable to both homesteaders and ranchers. By the early 1900s cooking for summer haying crews and fall threshing crews, in addition to normal fall roundups and spring brandings, added to the ranch cooks' duties. With the advent of the Rural Electrification Program in the 1930s, some ranch cooks traded their old wood ranges for new-fangled electric stoves, which gave them more time to cook rather than wipe perspiration from their foreheads as they prepared meals during the summer heat. Along with the electric ranges came refrigerators. Gone were the worries about food spoilage and the ability to keep fresh produce for an extended time. Those ranch cooks were just as savvy as the chuck wagon cookies of the mid-1800s. They quickly figured out ways to improve the grub and send the cowboys off to the bunkhouse with full bellies and grins.

We don't need to pore through historical accounts of that era or rent the 1989 movie *Lonesome Dove* to learn more about cowboy cooking. Today, chuck wagon cooking draws huge crowds at various Western Heritage and ranch rodeos throughout the west. At these events you can watch today's cowboys in period dress cooking alongside authentic chuck wagons using the same Dutch ovens, skillets, and camp gear those early ranch and cowboy cooks used in the nineteenth century. You'll see Dutch ovens covered with mesquite coals next to campfires with old-time coffee pots suspended from tripods. The tantalizing odors of simmering briskets, cowboy beans, and peach cobblers plus the subtle smell of camp coffee continue to mesmerize the crowds even today.

The recipes I've included come from many sources. Some are old family favorites, some are from friends, some have languished in my files for years, and some come straight from my childhood memories. In one way or another, all can be traced to a time when cows and cowboys were the dominant force in the American West. Access to ingredients old-time cooks never had would classify many recipes as exotic . . . . but trust me, they wouldn't have sneered at progress that had made dinner turn out just a little better.

TALKIN' THE TALK

Branding: Usually occurs in the spring when calves are rounded up, marked with a hot iron, dehorned, castrated, and vaccinated; followed by ranch cookin' typically featuring Rocky Mountain Oysters.

Bunkhouse: Cowboy dormitory usually featuring a woodstove and coffee can spittoons.

Camp coffee: Coffee grounds and water simmered over a wood fire.

Chips: Dried cow pies used in lieu of wood for cooking fuel; also known as cowboy charcoal.

Chuck: Food, grub, vittles, etc.

Chuck box: A box or container for the chuck.

Chuck wagon: A horse-drawn mobile kitchen used on trail drives and ranch roundups.

Cook or cookie: The designated cook on a ranch or trail drive.

Dutch oven: A three-legged cast-iron pot with a flanged lid for holding hot coals.

Drag: Riding behind the herd to prevent stragglers from leaving the herd . . . a very dusty and dirty job.

Fly: Canvas awning rigged over the tailgate of the chuck wagon to provide shade or shelter.

Goncho: Steel rod used to lift hot lids from Dutch ovens.

Line shack: Remote cabin used to house cowboys when working far from the home ranch.

Pair: Two cards of the same kind in a poker hand, or a cow and her calf.

Remuda: Spare horses accompanying a trail drive or roundup so cowboys could swap a tired horse for a fresh one.

Rocky Mountain Oysters: Calf testicles fried and served at brandings and other ranch events.

Roundup: Typically occurs when cattle are gathered to a central location for branding, shipping, etc.

Slick: An unbranded cow or calf.

Tow sack: A large burlap bag, or gunnysack, used for easy storage on the trail.

Tripod: Three metal rods connected at the top with a short piece of chain used to hang coffee pots and other cookware over a campfire.

Wrangler: The guy whose job it was to take care of the horse herd that accompanied a crew of cowboys on a trail drive or roundup.

USING A DUTCH OVEN

*T*he Dutch oven has been part of the American cooking scene since Colonial times. Its basic design has stood the test of time: a three-legged cast-iron pot with a flanged lid that allows wood coals or charcoal briquets to be held on it. The legs and lid set the oven apart from other cooking pots and contribute to its versatility. The legs allow the oven to sit on a bed of coals and still be high enough so the coals are not snuffed out from lack of oxygen. The lid allows additional coals, and therefore additional heat, to be put on the top. Thus, much like our kitchen ovens of today with their top and bottom elements, the Dutch oven has the versatility of both top and bottom heat sources. The surrounding heat is what creates the true oven effect and allows outdoor cooks to quickly and simply prepare out-of-this-world meals either on their patios or deep in the backwoods.

In addition to operating as an oven, the versatile Dutch oven can be used as a soup pot, frying pan, deep fryer, and more. Whether using wood coals, charcoal briquets, or a modern camp stove for heating, the lid can be placed over the heat and used as a shallow skillet or griddle. One-pot cooking takes on new meaning for the versatile Dutch oven, even for a beginning cook!

Like any other endeavor, the right equipment makes the job easier:

1. Firepan or steel cooking table to contain wood coals or briquets

2. Lid lifter

3. Metal tongs at least 12 inches long for arranging briquets

4. Pair of heavy leather gloves for handling hot pots

5. Small camp-type shovel for transferring briquets or wood coals

6. Metal container such as a military surplus ammo can to dispose of spent ashes

Dutch ovens come in a variety of sizes and are described by both their diameter and their capacity, or liquid volume. They range in size from 5 inches in diameter to 23-inch behemoths weighing more than 50 pounds empty. Originally, all Dutch ovens were made of cast iron, but now they are available in cast aluminum and weigh about one-third of what an equivalent iron oven weighs. If a standard size exists, most cooks would consider the 12-inch 6-quart Dutch oven to be the one. Because most recipes call for this size oven, it's a good size to start with. As cooking skills increase or you start cooking for large groups, you can choose from a variety of oven sizes.

There are several good commercial firepans and cooking tables, but a metal wheelbarrow, oil change pan, or even a metal garbage can lid set on bricks or cinder blocks will work. You just need something to safely contain the hot briquets as they burn — for fire safety and also in case of wind. A good lid lifter is the number-one accessory. You need to easily and safely pick up the lid not only to check on the progress of the dish but also to dump the lid's hot coals into the ash container at serving time. All Dutch oven cooks flavor meals with ash when they lift the lid, but a good lifter will reduce that problem.

Heat management rather than recipe preparation is the real key to successful Dutch oven cooking.

A gourmet meal at home can be burned as easily through improper heat management as a meal

Baking, bottom heat:

For a 12-inch oven, use five or six briquets spaced evenly in a circle slightly less than the diameter of the oven, with two or three spaced evenly in the center. Only enough heat to brown the biscuits or corn bread is needed underneath.

Baking, top heat:

Place briquets next to each other around the outside flange of the lid, with two or three spaced evenly around the lid handle. You'll need about 18 to 24 briquets, which provide the high temperatures needed to bake and brown bread, biscuits, desserts, and so on.

Roasting:

Use the same heat you use for baking. If the dish has cooking liquid, increase the number of briquets underneath by up to 50 percent.

cooked over wood coals on a family camping trip. For beginning cooks, I suggest starting with a recipe you're familiar with, even if it's just heating up a couple of cans of stew.

In the kitchen, heat management consists merely of twisting the proper knob to the desired temperature. In Dutch oven cooking, however, you must place the correct number of live coals or briquets underneath the oven. (For our purposes we'll talk about charcoal briquets because briquets are what most beginners will feel most comfortable using.) Briquets should be lit about 15 to 20 minutes prior to cooking and should be turning light gray when they are ready to use. Unless there is wind, the briquets should last for about an hour. Most dishes will cook in that amount of time. However, for large roasts plan on adding fresh briquets every hour.

Frying/Boiling:

Place enough briquets underneath to achieve the desired temperature.

...thod is to use what I call the smell test: "If it smells done, it's done. If it smells burnt, it's burnt. And if you can't smell it, it's not done!"

When I was a little kid, my idea of an appetizer meant sneaking a couple of chocolate chip cookies out of Mom's cookie jar a few minutes before dinner. Obviously, times and attitudes change. Though a fair amount of information was recorded about life on trail drives and ranches in the mid-1800s, cooking and eating were peripheral issues. Why? Because fillin' one's belly came secondary to the main job of the day. In other words, the cowboys and ranchers considered cookin' and eatin' a basic necessity not worthy of much mention when compared to the job of getting a herd of Texas Longhorns to the railroads

FIXIN' TO EAT

of Abilene or Dodge City, or rounding up stock from the mesquite scrub country of West Texas. So, for the most part, we have to rely on what little has been written about appetizers on the trail and on our own intuition.

It's just a guess, based on my experience of regularly spending three weeks on horseback in the Idaho wilderness, that leftovers from one day's meals would figure prominently as the next day's appetizers or in the next day's meal plans. Imagine the following scene: It's late afternoon when a cowboy rides into camp to get a fresh horse from the ramuda. Cookie has a pot of beans simmering over a buffalo-chip fire for the evening meal. The cowboy knows that

dinner is several hours away, but the smell of beans cooking starts his belly growling. Being on good terms with the cookie, he asks for something to tide him over until he gets back for supper. The cookie rustles up a couple of yesterday's sourdough biscuits out of a tow sack and ladles some of the pot liquor off the beans onto a tin plate before sending off the cowpoke to rejoin the herd. Voila! An appetizer is born!

As with any person who regularly performs hard physical work, working cowboys require a bit more fuel than those of us who make a living in front of a computer screen. Snacks prepared for hungry cowpokes started a culinary trend. In the

intervening years, appetizers have become a tradition both in restaurants and at home.

The appetizers I've included reflect some of the savvy of old-time chuck wagon and ranch cooks. For example, when you fry bacon for breakfast, fry enough for Shrimp 'n' Bacon Bites to serve just before dinner. If breakfast includes soft-boiled eggs, hard boil enough extras for Deviled Eggs. Depending on the crowd you're cooking for, you may want to have prepared appetizers on hand. A bowl of Texas Caviar, a few soda crackers or some corn bread, and a bottle of pepper sauce for some extra zip will keep folks visiting around the dinner table while you finish preparing supper.

Texas Caviar

SERVES 18 TO 24

2 15-oz. cans black-eyed peas,
   drained (not rinsed)
1 cup salad oil
1/4 cup red wine vinegar
1/2 cup onion, thinly sliced
   (use small boiling-type onions, if available)
1/2 tsp salt
2 cloves garlic, whole or finely minced
cracked pepper to taste

*M*ix all ingredients well and pour in jar. Let marinate in refrigerator 2 weeks befo serving. Remove garlic if using whole cloves. Serve with freshly baked corn bread.

18

Stuffed Celery Sticks

7 medium stalks celery,
   well dried
1/2 cup Swiss cheese,
   grated
1/2 cup cooked ham,
   finely chopped
1/3 cup mayonnaise or
   salad dressing
1/2 tsp prepared mustard

Cut celery into 3-inch pieces. Mix remaining ingredients. Spread about 1 tablespoon in each celery stalk. Cover and refrigerate 1 hour before serving.

SERVES 18 TO 24

Party Sandwiches

Be creative and be your own caterer!
By mixing and matching different bread
flavors, types, sizes, and colors with
several toppings, party sandwiches
can be a colorful and delightful
addition to any event or party.

Cutting Bread:

Trim crusts from different types
of sliced bread and cut squares.
Cut various shapes from each
square piece: cut pieces
diagonally to make triangles;
quarter square pieces to make
smaller squares; or cut squares
in half, then lengthwise in half
again to make four rectangular
pieces from each square.

Toppings and Spreads:

Use many spreads for party
sandwiches. It is easiest to use a
variety of cheese spreads from
the dairy case. Top breads
with slices of black olives or
pimento-stuffed green olives.
For fancier variations, try the
rootin'-tootin' spreads on
pages 21–23.

EACH SPREAD MAKES 12

Olive Nut Spread

4 oz. cream cheese, softened
1/2 cup walnuts, finely chopped
1/4 cup pimento-stuffed green olives, chopped
2 tbsps milk

Mix all ingredients and spread on breads.
Chill before serving.

Shrimp Salad Spread

1 6-oz. can shrimp, rinsed
    and drained
1 hard-boiled egg, finely chopped
2 tbsps celery, finely chopped
1 tbsp lemon juice
1/8 tsp salt
dash pepper
3 tbsps mayonnaise or
    salad dressing

Mix all ingredients and
spread on breads.
Chill before serving.

Deviled Ham Spread

1 4-oz. can deviled ham
1/4 cup sour cream
2 tbsps sweet pickle relish, drained
1 tbsp onion, grated
dash pepper sauce

Mix all ingredients and spread on breads. Chill before serving.

Chicken, Ham, and Cheese Spread

1 5-oz. can boned chicken, rinsed and finely chopped
1/2 cup cooked ham, finely chopped

1/2 cup sharp cheddar cheese, grated
1 tsp salt

dash pepper
1 tbsp parsley, chopped

Mix chicken, ham, cheese, salt, and pepper. Spread on breads and sprinkle parsley on top. Chill before serving.

Clam and Cream Cheese Spread

4 oz. cream cheese, softened
1 4-oz. can minced clams, drained and rinsed
4 tsps seasoned salt
1/4 tsp Worcestershire sauce
1/8 tsp onion juice

Mix all ingredients and spread on breads. Chill before serving.

Smoked Turkey Spread

3 oz. smoked sliced turkey, finely chopped
1/4 cup celery, finely chopped
1 tbsp onion, finely chopped
1/3 cup mayonnaise or salad dressing
1/8 tsp liquid smoke

Mix all ingredients and spread on breads.
Chill before serving.

Crabmeat Spread

1 7-oz. can crabmeat, drained and
    cartilage removed
1/3 cup mayonnaise or salad dressing
1 tbsp capers, plus more for garnish

Mix crabmeat, mayonnaise, and 1 tablespoon capers;
spread on breads. Add capers for garnish.
Chill before serving.

Rocky Mountain Oysters

12 medium or 24 small Rocky
Mountain Oysters
6 eggs
3 cups crushed cracker crumbs
oil
salt and pepper

 f using medium oysters, cut in half. Beat eggs until just blended. Dip oysters in eggs and roll in cracker crumbs. Heat oil and sauté oysters on high heat until brown. Place on cookie sheet and season with salt and pepper. Bake at 350 degrees 20 minutes.

MAKES 1 TO 2 DOZEN

24

Rib-Stickin' Dip

8 oz. cream cheese
4 oz. sour cream
3 tbsps blue cheese dressing
3 large pimento-stuffed green olives
3 green onions, diced
black pepper
crushed red pepper
garlic powder
crackers or celery sticks

Mix cream cheese, sour cream, dressing, olives, and onions and season to taste with black pepper, red pepper, and garlic powder. Refrigerate at least 1/2 hour. Serve on crackers or celery sticks.

SERVES 6

Onion Rings

1 large Vidalia onion
1 quart buttermilk
2 cups flour
cooking oil

SERVES 2

Slice onion and separate into rings. Cover with buttermilk and let stand 1 hour. Put flour in plastic or paper bag. Add onion rings, inflate bag, and shake until rings are coated with flour. Fry in hot oil and drain on paper towels.

Cheese Straws

2 cups flour
1 tsp salt
2/3 cup butter
1/3 to 1/2 cup
   ice water

2/3 cup American
   cheese, grated
   and divided
paprika

$\mathcal{S}$ift flour and salt, cut in butter, and add enough water to hold dough together. Turn onto lightly floured board and roll into oblong shape. Sprinkle half the dough with some cheese and paprika. Fold over two or three times and roll out. Repeat until all cheese is used. Roll slightly thinner than pie pastry. Cut into tiny circles or 4-inch-long sticks. Bake on ungreased cookie sheet at 425 degrees 7–10 minutes.

MAKES 18 TO 24 APPETIZERS

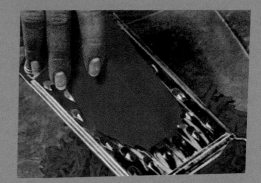

Cheese Appetizers

1/2 cup aged
   American cheese, grated
1/2 tsp salt
1 tsp flour
1 egg white, stiffly beaten
12 saltine crackers

$\mathcal{C}$ombine cheese, salt, and flour. Fold in egg white. Drop 1 teaspoon mixture on each cracker. Bake at 400 degrees 10 minutes.

MAKES 12 APPETIZERS

Hot Mustard and Sausage

1 1/3 cups (4-oz. can) dry
    mustard (Colman's if available)
2 tbsps sugar
2 tsps salt
1/4 cup oil

1/2 cup wine vinegar
cooked meats
    (sausage, Chinese roast pork,
    corned beef, corned venison)

Combine mustard, sugar, salt, oil, and vinegar, blending well. Refrigerate. Dip thin slices of meat, hot or chilled, into mixture. Toasted sesame seeds can also be served for dipping. (NOTE: Stores well in refrigerator for several months.)

MAKES ABOUT 2 CUPS

Little Wiener Kabobs

30 cocktail wieners
15 skewers
4 dill pickles, cut into 3/4-inch pieces (about 3/4 cup)
1 4-oz. can button mushrooms, drained
1 pint small cherry tomatoes

15 large pimento-stuffed green olives
1 medium green pepper, cut into 3/4-inch squares (about 30 pieces)
2 tbsps butter
1 tsp lemon juice
red pepper sauce

*P*reheat oven to 450 degrees. Alternate 2 wieners with vegetables on each skewer. Place on rack in broiler pan. Heat butter, lemon juice, and hot sauce until butter is melted. Brush skewers with lemon-butter mixture. Bake until hot, 4–6 minutes.

MAKES 14 TO 15 KABOBS

6 hard-boiled eggs,
   peeled
1/2 tsp salt
1/2 tsp dry mustard
1/4 tsp pepper
3 tbsps mayonnaise
   or salad dressing
2 tbsps vinegar or
   pickle juice
paprika

Deviled Eggs

Cut eggs lengthwise into halves. Slip yolks into bowl and mash with fork. Add salt, mustard, pepper, mayonnaise, and vinegar and mix thoroughly. Fill egg whites with egg yolk mixture, heaping slightly. Arrange eggs on serving plate. Lightly sprinkle paprika on eggs for color. Cover and refrigerate no longer than 24 hours.

MAKES 12

8 oz. cream cheese
4 oz. blue cheese
1 cup sharp cheddar cheese, grated
1/4 cup onion, finely chopped
1 tbsp Worcestershire sauce
3/4 cup nuts, chopped

Party Cheese Ball

*P*lace cheeses in small mixing bowl. Let stand at room temperature until softened. Beat in onion and Worcestershire sauce on low speed. Beat on medium speed, scraping bowl frequently, until fluffy. Cover and refrigerate at least 8 hours. Shape mixture into 1 large ball or about 3 dozen 1-inch balls. Roll in chopped nuts and place on serving plate. Cover and refrigerate until firm, about 2 hours. To serve small balls, insert wooden pick in each.

SERVES 2 TO 3 DOZEN

Olive Cheese Balls

2 cups sharp cheddar
   cheese, shredded
1 1/4 cups flour

1/2 cup butter or margarine, melted
3 to 4 dozen small pimento-stuffed
   green olives, drained

*M*ix cheese and flour; mix in butter. Work dough with hands if it seems dry. Mold 1 teaspoon dough around each olive, shaping into ball. Place balls 2 inches apart on ungreased cookie sheet. Cover and refrigerate at least 1 hour. Preheat oven to 400 degrees. Bake until set, about 15-20 minutes.

MAKES 3 TO 4 DOZEN

MAKES 16 TO 20

Shrimp 'n' Bacon Bites

1 cup cooked shrimp,
   cleaned
1/2 clove garlic, slivered
1/2 cup chili sauce
8 to 10 slices bacon

Mix shrimp, garlic, and chili sauce.
Cover and refrigerate, stirring occasionally,
for several hours. Cut the bacon strips in half
widthwise. Fry bacon until partially cooked;
drain. Wrap each shrimp in bacon piece,
securing with wooden pick. Preheat oven to
broil at 550 degrees. Broil 2–3 inches from
heat until bacon is crisp.

Cocktail Meatballs

1 pound hamburger
1/2 cup dry breadcrumbs
1/3 cup onion, finely chopped
1/4 cup milk
1 egg
1 tbsp parsley, chopped
1 tsp salt
1/2 tsp Worcestershire sauce
1/8 tsp pepper
1/4 cup shortening
1 12-oz. bottle chili sauce
1 10-oz. jar grape jelly

Mix together hamburger, breadcrumbs, onion, milk, egg, parsley, salt, Worcestershire sauce, and pepper. Gently shape into 1-inch balls. Cook meatballs in shortening in skillet until brown. Remove meatballs from skillet; drain fat. Heat chili sauce and jelly in skillet, stirring constantly until jelly is melted. Add meatballs and stir until coated. Simmer uncovered 30 minutes. Serve hot in chafing dish.

MAKES 4 TO 5 DOZEN

The tantalizing aroma of fresh-baked bread ranks among the most recognizable smells in the world. Whether it's Pan de Campo (Mexican camp bread) baked in a Dutch oven over a bed of mesquite coals or crusty Italian loaves baked in a brick oven, the smell provokes the universal response of eyes closed, head tilted back, and a mouth-watering smile on the lips. Many a night a cowboy heading back to the chuck wagon or ranch nudged his cow pony into a faster gait when the wafting odor of fresh bread permeated the night air!

In the heyday of the American West, a cow boss whose cookie served fresh bread with every meal enjoyed bragging rights over outfits where the grub consisted of only beef and beans. Because the success of any outfit depended in large part upon the skill of the cowboys the cow boss hired, I can imagine a cow boss bragging about his cookie's biscuits when trying to attract a top hand away from a rival outfit! A cookie who believed that bread was the staff of life never worried about job security.

Although the collision between European and Native American cultures during westward expansion caused a lot of heartache and grief, there were many positive aspects, too. Second in importance only to firearms, metal cookware Native Americans obtained in trade with the white man revolutionized the way they cooked. They also realized that white man's flour made a great addition to their diet. Conversely, bannock and fry bread were two crossover hits

BOOT-SCOOTIN' BREADS

from the Native American menu to the cookie's menu cowboys still enjoy today.

The Mexican vaqueros, who played such an important role in the American West, brought a couple of their breads to ranch and chuck wagon cooks: Pan de Campo, which resembles a large leavened tortilla, and tortillas. Some folks may look down their noses at the lowly tortilla, but take it from me: a chunk of roast beef with some mustard and mayo rolled up in a tortilla will survive a lot longer in the saddlebags than a sandwich made with store-bought sliced bread.

The ranch cooks of today enjoy many technological advances, such as propane camp stoves, when they're cooking for a crew far from the home ranch. But, until someone invents a bread machine that can be plugged into a currant bush out on the range, bread served to the buckaroos will come from Dutch ovens heated with wood coals!

Scratch Biscuits

2 cups flour
1 tbsp baking powder
1/8 tsp salt
1/3 cup vegetable oil
2/3 cup buttermilk

Mix dry ingredients. Add liquid ingredients. Stir in bowl or work with hands just to form a ball. Do not knead. For moister dough, add a little more buttermilk. Pat on floured board to 3/4-inch thickness. Cut the biscuits to desired size and place touching in bottom of 10-inch Dutch oven. Cover. Place 4–6 briquets under oven, 15–18 briquets around outside edge of lid, and about 3 briquets spaced evenly in center of lid. Bake about 20–25 minutes until brown. To bake in 12-inch Dutch oven, place biscuits touching in bottom. Bake with 6–7 briquets under oven, 18–21 briquets on the outside edge of lid, and about 3 briquets spaced evenly in center of lid. To bake in conventional oven, place biscuits in cast-iron skillet or lightly greased cookie sheet. Bake at 425 degrees 20–25 minutes. (NOTE: This recipe doubles or triples easily. A double batch fits just right in a 16-inch Dutch oven, using 8–10 briquets under the oven and rimming the lid with briquets.)

Variations:

PLAIN DUMPLINGS: Increase milk to 1 cup

HERB BISCUITS: Add 3/4 teaspoon Italian seasoning

CHICKEN DUMPLINGS: Add 1/2 teaspoon poultry seasoning to flour

BEEF OR VENISON DUMPLINGS: Add 1 heaping tablespoon prepared horseradish to liquids

SERVES 4 TO 6

Bannock Fry Bread

1 cup flour
1 tsp baking powder
1 tsp sugar
1 tsp lard or
   shortening

1/2 cup water
willow sticks
butter or shortening

Mix dry ingredients and cut in shortening. Add water slowly until dough is slightly tacky. Knead just long enough to form into a ball. Pinch off ping pong ball-sized pieces of dough and roll into strips about 1/2-inch wide and 8–10 inches long or however long they turn out to be. Peel bark off willow stick as if roasting marshmallows. Dry peeled portion well with hand towel and wipe with a little butter. Put end of stick through one end of dough strip. Wrap rest of dough around stick. At end of stick, pinch dough back on itself to help keep it on stick. Toast over coals until dough rises a little and turns golden brown.

SERVES 4 TO 6

Fry Bread

2 cups flour
1 tsp baking powder
1 tsp salt
2 tbsps shortening

3/4 cup
  warm water
hot oil

Mix dry ingredients together and cut in shortening. Add water a little at a time until soft dough forms. It shouldn't stick to hands and should have slight shine or glisten. Knead 2 minutes. Pinch off golf ball-size pieces and roll on floured cutting board until size of salad plate. Fry in hot oil until bubbles start to form, turn over. If bubbles get too big, pop with spatula or fork. Serve with butter and honey or use as flour tortilla with scrambled eggs or other dishes.

SERVES 6 TO 8

Refrigerator Rolls

2 cups boiling water
1/2 cup sugar
2 tsps salt
3 tbsps shortening
2 pkgs active dry yeast
1/4 cup lukewarm water
7 cups flour

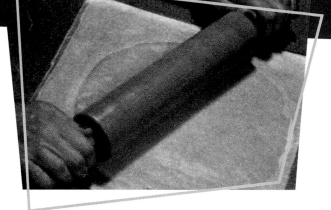

Place boiling water, sugar, salt, and shortening in large bowl. Let stand until lukewarm. In separate bowl, dissolve yeast in lukewarm water. Add dissolved yeast to sugar mixture. Gradually add flour. Knead well. If using immediately, let rise until double, punch down, then pinch or roll into golf ball-size pieces and place in greased pan. Bake at 400 degrees until brown, about 20-25 minutes. If not using immediately, put bowl of dough in refrigerator after kneading. It will keep up to 7 days if kept covered. It may be necessary to punch down dough as it chills. When ready to make rolls, let dough rise in warm place until doubled, punch down, then form balls and bake as above.

MAKES ABOUT 2 DOZEN

Hush Puppies

1 1/2 cups white cornmeal
1/4 cup sifted flour
2 tsps baking powder
1 tsp sugar
1 tsp salt
3 tbsps green onion, grated or finely diced
1 egg, beaten
3/4 cup milk or buttermilk

MAKES 15 TO 18

Mix first five ingredients together; set aside. Combine onion, egg, and buttermilk and stir. Add to dry ingredients and mix well. Drop by spoonfuls into hot fat, about 375 degrees and 1-1 1/2 inches deep. Turn once or cook until hush puppy floats.

Angel Biscuts

*D*issolve yeast in warm water with sugar (called "proofing the yeast"; it gets a bit foamy). Mix dry ingredients well; add shortening, yeast mixture, and buttermilk. Knead on floured surface. Don't overwork. Pat out on floured surface and cut to desired size. Preheat Dutch oven with 5–7 briquets underneath and 20–24 on top. I use Crisco to grease bottom of oven and a little pat on top of each biscuit. Bake at 375 degrees for 20–30 minutes. You don't have to let them rise first. (NOTE: The dough keeps well in the cooler or the refrigerator; legend has it up to six weeks. I honestly don't know that because they usually get eaten in two or three days. At home I bake on a preheated round cast-iron griddle in the oven at 375 degrees for 20–30 minutes until golden brown.

1 pkg dry yeast
2 tbsps warm water
3 tbsps sugar
5 cups flour
1 tsp soda
1 tsp salt
3 tsps baking powder
2/3 cup shortening
2 cups buttermilk

SERVES 16 TO 18

Buttermilk Cornbread

SERVES 6 TO 8

1 egg
2 cups buttermilk
1 1/3 cups cornmeal
1/2 cup flour
1 tsp baking soda

2 tsps baking powder
2 tbsps sugar
1 tsp salt
3 tbsps hot bacon drippings, oil, or shortening

Beat egg then add buttermilk. Mix dry ingredients and add to buttermilk mixture. Pour in drippings and stir. Preheat 12-inch Dutch oven 15 minutes with 10 briquets under oven and 22–24 briquets on outside edge of lid. Add batter and reduce number of briquets underneath to 5–7 and bake about 35–45 minutes. To bake in conventional oven, pour into hot, greased pan (9 x 13-inch or smaller for thicker bread). Bake at 425 degrees 30 minutes.

Butter Horns

Powdered sugar frosting:

2 cups powdered sugar (approximate)
1/4 tsp salt
3 tbsps butter
2 tbsps cream
1 tsp vanilla

Measure all ingredients into small bowl. Beat with mixer or by hand until creamy and thick enough to spread.

Add butter, sugar, and salt to milk. Cool to lukewarm. Add yeast, let stand 3 minutes. Add 2 cups flour. Beat well. Add eggs then remaining flour. Knead until smooth. Let rise to twice its bulk. Divide dough into about 40 golf ball-size buns. Roll each piece into triangular shape about 3 inches on each side. Roll with fingertips from long side to center and form into crescent. Place on buttered baking sheet and let rise for about 30–40 minutes. Bake at 425 degrees 20–30 minutes. Spread powdered sugar frosting on tops while warm, if desired.

1 cup butter
1/2 cup sugar
1 tsp salt
1 cup milk, scalded
1 cake compressed yeast, crumbled
4 1/2 cups flour, divided (approximate)
2 eggs
powdered sugar frosting (optional)

MAKES ABOUT 40

Prune Bread

Sift together flour, baking powder, soda, sugar, and salt. Add graham flour, candied fruit, if desired, and nuts. Add remaining ingredients, mixing just enough to moisten. Butter two loaf pans and bake at 350 degrees 45-55 minutes.

2 cups flour
1/2 tsp baking powder
1 tsp soda
1 cup sugar
1 tsp salt
2 cups graham flour
1 1/2 cups candied fruit (optional)
1 cup nuts, chopped to desired size
1 egg, beaten
1 1/2 cups sour milk or buttermilk
3/4 cup prune juice
2 tbsps butter, melted
1 cup stewed prunes

SERVES 8 TO 10

Orange Raisin Muffins

2 cups flour
1/3 cup sugar
3/4 tsp baking soda
1/2 tsp salt
1/2 cup seedless raisins
1/2 tsp orange rind, grated
1/3 cup orange juice
1 egg, well beaten
2/3 cup buttermilk
1/3 cup butter, melted

Sift dry ingredients together three times. Add raisins and orange rind. Combine liquid ingredients and add to dry mixture. Mix just enough to moisten. Fill buttered muffin pans two-thirds full. Bake at 400-425 degrees 25 minutes.

MAKES 12 TO 16

Cheese Popovers

1 cup flour
1/2 tsp salt
2 eggs, slightly beaten
1 cup milk
1 cup American cheese, grated

Sift flour and salt together. Combine eggs and milk; add to flour mixture. Beat mixture with egg beater until full of air bubbles. Drop 1 rounded teaspoon batter into each section of hot and well-buttered muffin pan. Cover each with 1 level tablespoon cheese, then cover with 1 teaspoon of batter. Bake at 425 degrees about 20 minutes; reduce heat to 350 degrees and bake 15–20 minutes.

SERVES 12 TO 16

43

Spoon Bread

$\mathscr{P}$reheat oven to 375 degrees. In top of double boiler over simmering water, scald milk. Beat egg yolks until thick and lemon colored; set aside. When milk is scalded, very gradually add cornmeal, stirring constantly. Stir until mixture thickens and becomes smooth. Remove from simmering water. Quickly and thoroughly blend mixture into egg yolks. Add butter, sugar, and salt; blend thoroughly. In separate mixing bowl use clean beaters to beat egg whites until rounded peaks form. Spread egg yolk and cornmeal mixture over egg whites and gently fold together. Turn into well-greased 2-quart casserole. Bake 35–40 minutes or until wooden pick or cake tester comes out clean when inserted into center.

2 cups milk
4 eggs, separated
1 cup white cornmeal
1/4 cup butter or
   margarine, softened
1 tbsp sugar
1/2 tsp salt

SERVES 6 TO 8

44

Wheat-Free Cornbread or Muffins

ix together eggs, buttermilk, and vegetable oil in a medium-size mixing bowl. In a separate bowl combine cornmeal, salt, baking powder, and baking soda and stir into egg mixture. Pour into 12-inch Dutch oven, a well-greased 9-inch baking pan, or 12 greased muffin cups. Place Dutch oven in firepan with 5–6 briquets under the Dutch oven and 20–25 briquets on the lid; or bake in oven at 425 degrees. Bake for 30–35 minutes or until done. For sweeter cornbread, add 2–3 tablespoons sugar.

2 eggs, beaten
2 cups buttermilk
2 tbsps vegetable oil
2 cups cornmeal
1 tsp salt
2 tsps baking powder
1 tsp baking soda
2 to 3 tbsps sugar
    (optional)

Breakfast Scones

2 cups flour
2 tbsps sugar, plus more
    for dusting
1 tsp salt
3 tsps baking powder
2 tbsps butter or
    margarine
2 eggs, well beaten
cold water
milk

Sift flour, 2 tablespoons sugar, salt, and baking powder; cut in butter. Add eggs and enough water to make soft dough. Turn onto lightly floured cutting board and pat into sheet about an inch thick. Cut into rounds or squares. Brush with milk and dust with sugar. Bake at 450 degrees about 15 minutes.

MAKES 8

Corn Pone

PONE IS A SOUTHERN TERM MEANING MUFFINS BAKED WITHOUT A MUFFIN TIN.

2 cups cornmeal
1 tsp salt
2 tsps flour
2 tsps bacon grease
about 1 cup milk (enough to
    make a stiff batter)

*M*ix all ingredients together, then form pones by hand and put on greased baking sheet. Bake 12–15 minutes at 425 degrees.

MAKES ABOUT
1 1/2 DOZEN

VITTLES TO FILL YER MIDDLES

Whether punchin' cows on the open range or mending fences at the home ranch, cowboys looked forward to one of their few daily pleasures: the evening meal. After work was done and the horses were munching hay in the corral, cowboys could kick back for a few minutes while the cookie finished workin' his magic. In most instances they would head for a nearby creek or the horse trough to splash a little water on their faces and wash the day's dust from their hands before sitting down for supper.

Menus probably varied only by the cut of beef the cookie chose for the main dish. Boiled, stewed, fried, or roasted, it was served with a side of beans and bread or biscuits for mopping up the juices. If they were on a trail drive, cowboys often started the day with the same grub the cookie had reheated from the previous day's supper. At the home ranch, however, chances are the cookie had pancakes, eggs, and ham or bacon (from hogs raised at the ranch) for breakfast.

It's my guess that quantity of food was just as important as quality! Doing hard physical work from daylight to dark required rib-stickin' meals to keep the cowboys happy. A sharp cookie knew that the monotony of work coupled with the same food day after day would make the crew restless and cranky. So he did what all good cooks still do today: he used his creativity to improve the final product with what was at hand. Whether it was simply a few wild onions dug from a meadow or a judicious pinch from a hoard of spices, cowboy cooks were always on the lookout for ways to make things better.

The beef industry was a driving force in the expansion and settlement of the American West. The wide-open plains and frontier towns became as much a melting pot of cultures as the rest of the country. Mexican vaqueros, freed slaves, Native Americans, and immigrants from many European countries all contributed not only their work but also their culinary influences. Those influences can still be seen in ranch recipes today.

Most of today's working ranches enjoy all the modern conveniences of urban America, including kitchen appliances and refrigeration. But, there are still times when it's necessary to feed a crew a long way from the kitchen. Rather than hitching teams to chuck wagons, today's cowboy cooks load their Dutch ovens and other kitchen necessities into pickup trucks before heading out to do what they've been doing since those trail drives of old.

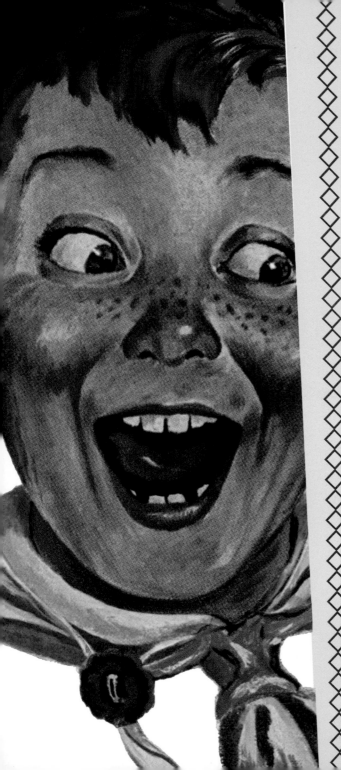

Homemade Hash and Wide Eyes

butter or margarine
6 cups or 3 15-oz. cans hash
6 eggs
salt and pepper (a dose of
  hot sauce works, too)

Melt dab of butter in 12-inch Dutch oven. Spoon in hash and spread evenly. Set oven in firepan with 5–6 briquets underneath; cook uncovered just until hash starts to bubble. While hash is heating, shovel lid full of coals from campfire or place 20–25 briquets on lid. Press coffee cup into hash to make 6 "nests." Break 1 egg into each nest and replace lid. Cook 6–8 minutes. Finished dish looks like a wide-eyed monster.

SERVES 3 TO 6

Potato Pancakes

2 cups raw potato, grated
1 tbsp onion, grated
2 eggs
4 tbsps flour
1 tsp salt
1/3 cup shortening

Combine potato, onion, eggs, flour, and salt. Heat shortening in frying pan. Drop mixture by tablespoons into pan. Flatten each cake with spatula. Fry until golden brown on each side.

SERVES 7 TO 8

Dutch Oven Layered Breakfast

butter
10 to 12 slices bread,
    trimmed and cubed
2 cups ham or sausage,
    cooked and diced

12 oz. sharp cheddar
    cheese, grated
6 to 7 eggs, lightly beaten
2 tbsps onion, minced

3 2/3 to 4 cups milk
1 tsp dry mustard
salt and pepper, to taste

Preheat 12-inch Dutch oven lid by rimming with 18–22 briquets. Butter oven; add bread, sprinkle meat over bread, and cover with cheese. Combine remaining ingredients and pour over cheese. Using 5–7 briquets under oven and briquets on lid, bake until knife inserted in center of mixture comes out clean. To bake in conventional oven, preheat to 325 degrees. Butter 9 x 13-inch baking dish; bake 1 hour.

SERVES 6 TO 8

4 to 6 tbsps olive or vegetable oil
6 to 8 baked potatoes
2 medium onions, diced
4 to 6 cloves garlic, minced

1/2 green or red bell pepper, chopped
salt, pepper, other seasonings, to taste
1 cup cheese, grated (optional)

Hearty Hashbrowns

Set 12-inch Dutch oven on propane stove over low to medium heat. Heat oil 2–3 minutes; add potatoes, onions, garlic, green pepper, and seasonings. Fry about 10 minutes until heated through. Sprinkle cheese on top and allow to melt, about 3 minutes. (Note: Diced-up leftover meat such as sausage, ham, or chicken can be added to make a one-dish breakfast.)

SERVES 4 TO 6

Bacon and Onion Potatoes

1 pound bacon, cut into small pieces
2 onions, diced
4 to 6 cloves garlic, minced

2 to 3 pounds potatoes, sliced
seasonings, to taste
1 pound cheddar cheese, grated

SERVES 8 TO 12

Brown bacon and onions in Dutch oven using 12–15 briquets under the oven. (Note: No briquets are needed on the lid when browning.) Drain some bacon grease. Add garlic; stir in potatoes. Using 5–6 briquets under oven and 14–16 on lid, cover and continue cooking 30–40 minutes or until potatoes are tender. Add cheese, melt, and serve.

54

Dutch Babies

3 eggs, well beaten
1/2 cup flour, sifted
1/2 tsp salt
1/2 cup milk
2 tbsps cold butter
powdered sugar
lemon juice

Blend eggs, flour, and salt. Add milk. Spread butter on sides and bottom of iron skillet. Pour batter into skillet. Bake uncovered at 425–450 degrees until lightly brown, about 15–18 minutes. To serve, dust with powdered sugar and sprinkle with lemon juice.

SERVES 4 TO 6

Rib-Stickin' Breakfast

1 pound ground beef or venison
2 tbsps oil
1 onion, diced
salt, pepper, other
    seasonings, to taste
12 eggs
1 4-oz. can diced jalapeños
    or green chiles

1 pound medium or sharp
    cheddar cheese, grated
    (Monterey Jack or Swiss
    can be substituted)
salsa (optional)
sour cream (optional)

In 12-inch Dutch oven over 8–10 briquets, or on a camp stove, brown meat in oil with onion and seasonings. Pour off excess fat. Add eggs and jalapeños to cooked meat. Stir over medium heat until eggs are nearly cooked. Sprinkle cheese over top. Remove from heat and let sit 2–3 minutes. Serve with salsa or sour cream, if desired.

SERVES 4 TO 6

Dutch Oven Omelet

1/2 cup canola or olive oil
24 extra-large eggs
1 cup milk
2 cups cooked meat: cubed ham or pork,
 crumbled bacon strips, country sausage,
 sausage link pieces, or leftover
 steak (or a mixture)
1 cup onions, diced or chopped
1 cup bell peppers (green, yellow, red), diced
1 cup mushrooms, sliced
1 to 2 fresh tomatoes, chopped
salt, pepper, hot sauce, other seasonings
1 stick butter, melted
2 cups cheddar cheese, grated, divided

SERVES 10 TO 12

Coat inside of 14-inch Dutch oven with oil. Break eggs into oven, add milk, and whip until thoroughly mixed. Stir in meat, onions, peppers, mushrooms, tomatoes, seasonings, butter, and 1 cup cheese. Cover and place on heat source. This meal is best cooked over camp stove or firebox for better temperature control. Low and slow is best. As eggs start to cook, stir frequently. As eggs set up, lower heat until fully cooked. In last few minutes before serving, spread remaining cup cheese over omelet, replace lid, and cook until cheese melts.

Forty-Mile Stew

SERVES 12

2 to 3 pounds round steak, cut into 1-inch cubes
1/4 cup olive or salad oil
1/2 pound mushrooms, sliced
3 pounds potatoes, sliced 1/3-inch thick
salt, pepper, other seasonings, steak sauce
2 large slicing tomatoes, sliced 1/3-inch thick
1/2 pound green peppers, julienned
1 large yellow onion, sliced 1/3-inch thick
2 pounds breakfast sausage made into patties
1 pound sharp cheddar cheese, sliced
thick (or Swiss or provolone)

In 12-inch Dutch oven using 15–18 briquets under oven or on camp stove, brown meat in oil. As meat finishes browning, throw in mushrooms. Remove from heat and make sure no meat has stuck to bottom. Layer potatoes over meat and mushrooms; add seasonings. In whatever order you like, layer tomatoes, peppers, and onion. Place sausage patties over top of last veggie. Bake slowly with 6–8 briquets under oven and 15–18 on lid. Add fresh briquets to top and bottom after 1 hour; cook 30–40 minutes. With only moisture that cooks out of vegetables for liquid, this ends up being more like casserole than stew. Add more liquid during cooking, if desired. Ten minutes before serving, remove briquets from lid, place cheese over sausage, and replace lid. Cheese will melt in about 5 minutes. Make sure to get part of each layer when serving.

1 pound round steak, cut into
   cubes or strips
1/4 cup flour
2 tbsps oil
1/2 cup onion, chopped
2 cloves garlic, minced
1 6-oz. can mushrooms with broth
1 cup sour cream
1 10 3/4-oz. can mushroom soup
1 tbsp Worcestershire sauce
1/2 tsp salt
1/8 tsp pepper
2 cups hot rice, cooked

Roll meat in flour and brown in hot oil in large skillet. Add onion, garlic, and mushrooms with broth. Cook until onions are tender or opaque. Add sour cream, mushroom soup, Worcestershire sauce, salt, and pepper and cook until thick and bubbly. Cover and simmer, stirring occasionally, about 1 hour or until meat is tender. Serve over hot rice.

Round Steak Stroganoff

SERVES 4 TO 6

Dutch Oven Pot Roast

2 tsps salt or favorite seasoning
1 5-pound round bone beef roast
2 tbsps shortening
1/2 cup barbecue sauce
1/2 cup apple cider
8 carrots, peeled and cut
   into 2-inch chunks
6 potatoes, peeled and quartered
2 onions, peeled and quartered
1 10-oz. package frozen okra or
   1/2 pound fresh okra cut
   into 1-inch pieces

Rub salt into meat. Melt shortening in 12-inch Dutch oven on top of stove and brown roast over medium heat, turning once. Reduce heat; pour barbecue sauce and cider over roast. Cover and simmer over medium heat about 2 hours. Add carrots, potatoes, and onions; cook 1 hour. Add okra 15–20 minutes before serving.

Chicken Fried Steak

2 pounds minute steaks or
    pounded beef filet
1 16-oz. can evaporated milk
1/4 cup flour, plus additional
    for dredging
salt and pepper, to taste
vegetable oil
    1/4 cup butter or margarine (optional)
    1 10 3/4-oz. can beef consommé
    1 tbsp sweet vermouth

SERVES 6

Tenderize meat (if desired), dip in milk, and then dip into flour seasoned with salt and pepper. Repeat once; reserve unused milk. Fry in 1-inch hot oil over medium-high heat until golden brown or to desired crispness. To make gravy, mix 1/4 cup browned drippings with 1/4 cup flour. If grease has been "cooked" too much and has turned a dark brown, use 1/4 cup butter to begin gravy instead of drippings and stir until thoroughly mixed. Add consommé and remainder of milk. Add more milk to establish your preference of gravy thickness. Bring mixture to very light boil; add vermouth, using more to taste if desired. DO NOT salt gravy! Consommé adds all the taste and salt you need, but you may wish to season with pepper. Serve gravy hot with fried steaks and mashed taters!

1 10 3/4-oz. can tomato
  soup, divided
1 1/2 pounds ground beef
1/2 cup fine bread crumbs
1/2 cup onion, finely chopped
1 egg
1 tsp salt
dash pepper
1 tbsp shortening
1/4 cup water
3/4 tsp horseradish

Stove-Top Meat Loaf

*T*horoughly mix 1/2 can soup with beef, bread crumbs, onion, egg, salt, and pepper. Firmly shape into two loaves. In skillet, brown loaves on both sides in shortening. Cover; cook over low heat 25 minutes. Spoon off fat. Top with remaining 1/2 can soup, water, and horseradish. Cook uncovered 10–15 minutes.

SERVES 6

Dogs in Blankets

10 cups oil
2 cups self-rising flour
1 egg
pinch salt
1 to 1 1/2 cups milk
1/2-inch slices cold
   roast beef

Heat oil in 12-inch Dutch oven using about 25 briquets under the oven. (Note: No need for briquets on top when frying.) Put flour, egg, and salt in bowl. Mix well, slowly adding a little milk at a time until batter is smooth. Dip meat slices into batter and drop into hot oil. Turn once. When brown, place on paper towels to drain; serve.

SERVES 6 TO 12

Quick-Fix Chicken

1 frying chicken, cut up
1/3 cup Heinz 57 sauce
2 tbsps Worcestershire
 sauce
2 tbsps lemon juice
paprika

Place chicken in 12-inch Dutch oven. Mix sauces and lemon juice. Brush over chicken. Sprinkle with paprika. Use 8 briquets underneath oven and 18–22 briquets on lid. Bake 50–60 minutes. To bake in conventional oven, layer chicken in single layer in baking dish. Cover and bake at 400 degrees until tender, about 50–60 minutes. Juice makes delicious gravy.

Liver and Onions

deer or elk liver sliced 1/4-inch thick
(enough to serve 4 to 5)
cold water
3 to 4 tbsps bacon drippings or oil
pepper and garlic salt, to taste
3 to 4 medium onions, sliced

$\mathcal{S}$oak liver overnight in cold
water. Heat oil in large cast-iron skillet. Add liver
and season with pepper and garlic salt. Turn liver
in 3–4 minutes. Cover with onion slices. Cover
and cook 5 minutes. Stir once or twice and serve.
(Note: Sliced heart can be substituted. Some like
to dredge liver slices in flour before frying.)

SERVES 4 TO 5

Hearty Hamburger Pie

1 medium onion, diced
2 tbsps vegetable oil
1 pound lean ground beef
2 4-oz. cans green chilies,
   diced
1 11-oz. can tomato soup
1 tsp salt
1/4 tsp oregano
1/2 cup Monterey Jack
   cheese, grated

Pie crust:

2 cups Bisquick-type
   baking mix
1/2 cup milk
1 tbsp water

In 12-inch Dutch oven over 10–12 briquets, sauté onion in oil 5 minutes. Crumble meat and lightly brown; add remaining ingredients except cheese. Allow mixture to simmer while making pie crust. To make pie crust, mix ingredients and work into soft dough. On sheet of wax paper pat dough into circle slightly smaller in diameter than oven. Place dough over top of mixture. Put 22–24 coals on lid, cover, and bake 20–30 minutes. Five minutes before serving, sprinkle cheese over top.

SERVES 6 TO 8

1 pound beef, elk, or venison burger

3 to 4 red potatoes, cut "the quicker you want to eat, the smaller you cut 'em"

1 onion, cut just like the taters

1/2 tsp pepper

1/4 tsp garlic powder or 2 to 3 cloves minced garlic

cooking liquid, water will do, one or two beers are even better, and Laser says that dark beer makes it best

3 to 4 slices Swiss cheese

Laser Stew

Get a fire or briquets going as soon as you can. Dump everything except cheese into 12-inch Dutch oven and cook until liquid is reduced by 1/2 to 3/4, using 6-8 briquets under the oven and 14-16 on the lid. Take off lid and place cheese over top. Let cook a few minutes or until you can't take it any longer, then serve. Reheat leftovers while you make coffee in the morning and voila! You've just experienced Wilderness Fast Food times two!

SERVES 4

Ham Loaves

2 eggs, beaten
1 cup saltine cracker crumbs
2/3 cup milk
dash freshly ground pepper
1 pound fully cooked ham, ground
1 pound fresh pork, ground
1 8 1/4-oz. can pineapple
   slices, drained
2 maraschino cherries, halved
1/2 cup brown sugar
1 tsp dry mustard
2 tbsps vinegar

Combine eggs, cracker crumbs, milk, and pepper. Add meats; mix well. In bottom of 7 1/2 x 3 3/4 x 2 1/4-inch loaf pan, arrange 2 slices pineapple and 2 cherry halves. Firmly press half the meat mixture into pan. Loosen sides with spatula. Unmold into 9 x 9 x 2-inch baking pan. Repeat with remaining pineapple, cherries, and meat mixture, unmolding second loaf into same pan. Cover electric skillet and preheat to 375 degrees. Place pan of meat loaves on low rack in skillet. Cover; bake with vent closed 70 minutes. Drain off fat. Combine brown sugar, mustard, and vinegar; spoon over meat. Cover; bake 10 minutes.

SERVES 8

Tuna and Potato Chip Casserole

4 tbsps butter
4 tbsps flour
1/4 tsp pepper
2 1/2 cups milk
2 6-oz. cans flaked tuna fish
2 cups potato chips, crushed
1 10 3/4-oz. can mushroom soup

Melt butter in saucepan; blend in flour and pepper. Gradually add milk. Cook mixture until it becomes thick white sauce. Place alternate layers of tuna fish, chips, soup, and white sauce in greased 1 1/2-quart casserole. Top with potato chip layer. Bake at 350 degrees 30 minutes.

SERVES 6

69

Sweet and Sour Short Ribs

1 cup flour
salt
pepper
1 1/2 to 2 pounds
   lean short ribs
1 onion, sliced
1/2 pound bacon,
   sliced
1 10 3/4-oz. can
   beef consommé

Sauce:

3/4 cup ketchup
2 tbsps vinegar
2 tbsps Worcestershire sauce
4 tbsps soy sauce
1/4 to 1/2 cup brown sugar
3/4 cup water

Season flour with salt and pepper to taste. Dredge ribs in seasoned flour and place in 12-inch Dutch oven with 6–8 briquets under oven and 18–20 briquets on lid. Lay onion then bacon over ribs. Bake about 2 hours. Change briquets about every hour. To bake in conventional oven, place ribs in roasting pan and bake at 350 degrees 2 hours. To make sauce, mix all ingredients together while ribs are baking. Pour sauce over ribs and bake 2 hours or until tender.

SERVES 6 TO 8

Deviled Hamburgers

1 pound ground meat
2 tbsps chili sauce
1 1/2 tsps prepared mustard
1 1/2 tsps prepared horseradish
1 tsp onion, minced
1 1/2 tsps Worcestershire sauce
1 tsp salt
pepper to taste
8 slices of bread or 4 hamburger
  buns cut into halves

Combine all ingredients
except bread and mix well.
Spread on bread and broil
about 8 minutes at moderate
heat until done. Serve
immediately.

SERVES 4

Ham and Noodle Bake

1 1/2 cups cooked ham, cubed
1/4 cup onion, chopped
1/8 tsp thyme leaves, crushed
2 tbsps butter
1 10 3/4-oz. can creamy chicken mushroom soup
3/4 cup water
1/4 tsp pepper
2 cups noodles, cooked
1 cup green beans, cooked and cut
1/2 cup sharp cheddar cheese, grated

SERVES 4

In saucepan brown ham and cook onion with thyme in butter until tender. Stir in remaining ingredients except cheese. Pour into 1 1/2-quart casserole. Cover and bake at 350 degrees 30 minutes or until hot. Stir. Top with cheese. Bake until cheese melts.

Mountain Rainbow Trout

6 large frozen or fresh trout,
   cleaned and heads removed
2/3 cup yellow cornmeal
1/4 cup flour
2 tsps salt
1/2 tsp paprika
shortening or bacon drippings

Thaw frozen fish; dry with paper towels. Combine cornmeal, flour, salt, and paprika. Coat fish in mixture. Heat shortening in skillet over hot coals until drop of water sizzles. Brown until fish flakes easily when tested with fork, about 4 minutes on each side. Do not overcook!

SERVES 6

RANCHERO

Tamale Pie

1 pound ground beef
1/2 cup onion, chopped
1/3 cup green pepper, chopped
1 to 3 cloves garlic, minced

1 tbsp salad oil
1 11-oz. can chili beef soup
1 16-oz. can Mexican-flavored diced tomatoes
1/3 cup ripe olives, sliced
2 tbsps chili powder

3 cups water, divided
1 cup cornmeal
1/2 tsp salt
butter
1 cup cheddar cheese, grated

Brown beef in skillet; add onion, green pepper, and garlic; cook until tender. Pour off fat. Stir in soup, tomatoes, olives, and chili powder. Cook over low heat 15 minutes, stirring occasionally. Meanwhile, bring 2 cups water to boil. Mix cornmeal with salt and remaining 1 cup water. Pour cornmeal mixture into boiling water, stirring constantly. Cook over medium heat until thickened, about 15 minutes, stirring occasionally. Butter bottom and sides of 2-quart shallow baking dish; line with cooked cornmeal. Fill with beef mixture. Bake 30 minutes at 350 degrees. Top with cheese. Bake until cheese melts.

SERVES 6

Wagon Wheel Tuna Bake

2 10 3/4-oz. cans cream of
   mushroom soup
2 cups rice, cooked
1/3 cup milk
1 tbsp lemon juice

2 6-oz. cans tuna, drained and flaked
1 10-oz. pkg frozen broccoli spears,
   cooked and drained
1/2 cup cheddar cheese, grated

SERVES 4

In bowl combine soup, rice, milk, lemon juice, and tuna. Pour into 9-inch baking dish. Cover and bake at 400 degrees 20 minutes. Stir. Arrange broccoli in spokelike fashion on top. Sprinkle cheese on broccoli. Cover and bake 10 minutes.

Sloppy Joes

1 pound hamburger (moose
   or venison mixed with
   beef is great)
chopped onion (optional)
1 10 3/4-oz. can tomato soup
1/4 cup brown sugar
1 tbsp molasses
2 tsps Worcestershire sauce
2 tsps mustard
hamburger buns

Brown hamburger
and desired amount
of onion. Stir in
remaining ingredients
and heat through.
Serve on buns.

Join Up, Pardner...

76

SERVES 4 TO 6

Oven-Fried Chicken

1 fryer chicken, cut up
1/2 cup oil
1 egg, beaten
salt and pepper, to taste
3/4 cup bread crumbs

Preheat oven to 375 degrees. Wash chicken pieces and pat dry with paper towels. Roll pieces in oil. Dip in beaten egg. Season quickly with salt and pepper to taste before rolling chicken pieces in bread crumbs to coat both sides. Arrange pieces on a cooling rack placed on a greased cookie sheet. Bake for about an hour. A loose tent of foil placed over the chicken will hasten the baking process.

SERVES 4 TO 6

Stuffed Peppers

1 8 x 12-inch pan
    cornbread, baked
1 16-oz. can corn, drained
1 16-oz. can stewed
    tomatoes, chopped
1 16-oz. can peas, drained
1 to 2 pounds canned ham,
    cut into 1-inch squares
6 large bell peppers, cored
    and parboiled
6 strips bacon

Preheat oven to 300 degrees. Crumble cornbread into large mixing bowl. Add corn, tomatoes, and peas. Mix until evenly moist. Add ham and mix thoroughly. Stuff mixture into peppers and place in large baking dish or 12- to 14-inch Dutch oven. Spoon excess stuffing around peppers and place one strip bacon on top of each pepper. Place baking dish in oven and bake 40–50 minutes. If using Dutch oven, bake 40–50 minutes with 8 briquets under oven and 16–18 briquets on lid.

SERVES 6

Beanie Weenies

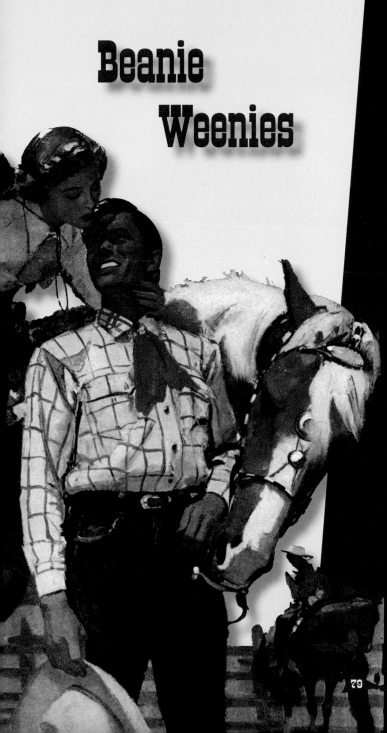

1 medium onion, diced
1 medium green pepper, diced
1 cup celery, diced
2 tbsps butter
1/2 pound ground beef
1 55-oz. can baked beans, drained
1 16-oz. pkg wieners
1 cup brown sugar
hot sauce or Tabasco

Sauté onion, green pepper, and celery in butter until onions are slightly opaque. Transfer mixture to 12-inch Dutch oven and set aside. Crumble and brown beef. Drain grease and transfer meat to green pepper mixture. Remove pork fat from beans; add beans to meat mixture. Cut wieners into bite-size pieces and add to mixture. Stir in brown sugar. Add hot sauce to taste. Heat thoroughly over low temperature with 5–7 briquets under oven and 16–18 on lid about 15–20 minutes; serve. To cook on conventional stove, transfer mixtures to large pot and heat thoroughly over low temperature 15–20 minutes.

SERVES 8 TO 12

79

SIX-SHOOTER SOUPS & SIDES

Ask any cowboy, old or young, and he'll tell you that a pot of beans simmered all day makes the perfect side dish for any meal, whether at home or on the range. Soups and stews that for years have been a mainstay in cow camps and line shacks taste just as good today as ever. Call it the nature of the beast, but cowboys — and cowgirls, for that matter — have always been interested in something that's quick, warm, and tasty! Whether it's a pot of pinto beans simmered with a ham hock or a hearty vegetable beef soup, cowboy cooks have always relied on a variety of side dishes to round out their menus.

Long before presentation became such an important part of today's culinary scene, ranch cooks inherently knew that the more variety in a meal, the more pleased the hungry bunch of cowpokes. It's my guess that the first time some grizzled old ranch cook added a few diced green chilies and pimentos to a can of corn, his goal was not to make it look pretty but simply to add some variety. Little did he know that by adding a few bits of color and subtle flavor to something as plain as a can of corn, he became a culinary trendsetter who would be imitated by hordes of TV cooks generations later.

To illustrate just how important soups and side dishes are, imagine for a moment an elegant prime rib dinner. Now, eliminate everything except the main course. It doesn't look like much, does it? A prime rib may get all the glory, but without au jus, garden veggies sautéed in butter, baked potato, and crusty dinner rolls, it's just another chunk of meat! For creative cooks, the arena of soups, stews, and side dishes is as wide as the open range. Take a lowly can of sauerkraut, and with just a few other simple ingredients they can turn it into Sauerkraut Soup or Sauerkraut Salad that folks will remember long after they've forgotten the meat loaf it was served with.

Many side dishes such as soups and stews can pull double duty as main courses. But a cup-size serving of Red Beans and Rice or Mushroom and Barley Soup also can make a great first course or side dish for nearly any meal. The old saying "Variety is the spice of life" is especially applicable when a cook's thoughts turn to "What's for dinner tonight?"

Soups and sides are also great starting points for novice cooks. Usually much simpler than entrées, these recipes are less intimidating than main courses, yet still leave beginning cooks with a great sense of confidence, pride, and accomplishment.

Ham Hock and Beans to Refrieds

1 cup beans, pinto
  or Anasazi
1 ham hock
1 yellow onion, chopped
8 cloves garlic, minced

pepper
garlic powder
onion powder
water
salt
butter or margarine

SERVES 6

If using pinto beans, soak overnight before cooking. Drain beans and put in 12-inch Dutch oven, or soup kettle, with ham, onion, garlic, pepper, garlic powder, and onion powder. Add water to cover ham hock and simmer several hours, covered, using 8 briquets under Dutch oven and 10–12 briquets on lid; change coals about every hour. Continue to simmer until meat cooks off bone and beans are tender. If using soup kettle, cover and simmer on stove for several hours to achieve same result. Remove all meat, skin, and bones. Separate meat from bones, skin, and fat. Chop meat and add to beans. Continue reducing liquid to desired consistency. Season with salt to taste. Serve with hot corn bread.

Refrieds:

Reduce liquid further. While cooking, mash beans and meat with potato masher to pasty consistency. Melt a few tablespoons butter into mixture. Add other ingredients such as more onions, salsa, and cumin. Continue to mash ingredients, cooking off liquid until desired consistency. Use as side dish or dip.

REFRIEDS SERVE 8 TO 10

Ham and Macaroni Salad

1/2 pound boiled or baked ham,
   cubed or diced
1/2 cup cheddar cheese,
   grated or cubed
2 cups elbow macaroni, cooked
1 cup celery, chopped
1 small onion, chopped
1/2 cup dill pickles, diced
1/2 cup mayonnaise
2 tsps mustard
lettuce leaves
3 tomatoes, quartered
6 hard-boiled eggs, sliced

Combine ham, cheese, macaroni, celery, onion, and pickles. In separate bowl mix mayonnaise and mustard, then stir into macaroni mixture, mixing well. Chill until ready to serve. Heap salad onto lettuce leaves. Garnish with tomatoes and eggs.

the joy of good eating

SERVES 6

Spuds and Onions Au Gratin

oil
2 to 3 pounds russet spuds,
   sliced as thin as you can
2 to 3 tbsps butter or
   margarine, melted
salt, pepper, other seasoning,
   to taste, divided

2 to 3 medium yellow onions,
   sliced thin
1 15-oz. can cheese soup
1/4 cup milk, divided
1/2 cup cracker or bread crumbs
   (seasoned if you wish)
1 cup cheddar cheese, grated

With paper towel wipe 12-inch Dutch oven with a little oil. Layer spuds in oven and brush with butter and some seasoning. Add layer of onions. Alternate layering spuds brushed with butter with onions. Thin soup with a little milk and pour over top. Sprinkle bread crumbs over; add additional seasoning. Set oven in firepan with 4–6 briquets underneath and 16–18 on lid. Bake 40–45 minutes. Remove oven from firepan and sprinkle cheese over bread crumbs. Let set about 5 minutes before serving.

SERVES 6 TO 8

Old-Fashioned Minestrone Soup

1 pound Italian dry beans or red
   kidney beans, or 2 15-oz. cans
   red kidney beans
4 cups water
3 pounds beef shanks
2 cups celery, chopped
1 medium yellow onion, diced
1 cup carrots, chopped
salt and pepper
1/4 pound salt pork, finely chopped
4 to 6 cloves garlic, minced
2 tbsps olive oil (optional)
hot sauce or Tabasco
2 cups zucchini, sliced
1 10-oz. pkg frozen Italian green beans
1 pound Napa cabbage, chopped
3 basil leaves, finely chopped
Parmesan or Romano cheese, grated

Soak dry beans overnight, then cook and put through blender or processor. Or drain canned beans and put through blender or processor. Add water to beef, celery, onion, carrots, salt, and pepper, and boil. Meanwhile, fry salt pork with garlic in olive oil, if necessary. Add hot sauce and fry slowly about 15 minutes. Add to beef and vegetable mixture. Add zucchini, green beans, cabbage, basil, and pureed beans 30 minutes before serving. Serve in bowls with cheese sprinkled over top.

SERVES 6 TO 8

1 pound dry pinto, Anasazi,
  or kidney beans
1 28-oz. can stewed tomatoes
1 28-oz. can tomato sauce
2 cups water
3 tbsps Mexican seasoning
1 tsp garlic powder
1/2 cup chili powder

1/2 tsp salt
1/2 tsp coarse ground pepper
2 large onions, cut in chunks
6 cloves garlic, sliced thin
2-3 tbsps olive oil
2 pounds ground venison
  or hamburger (coarse grind
  is heartier)

Basic Ranch Chili

Soak beans in large stock pot with enough water to cover plus another 4–5 inches. The next day, when you come back to camp for lunch, drain and rinse beans. Set 14-inch Dutch oven over 10–15 briquets and pour in beans, tomatoes, and tomato sauce. Add seasonings and onions. Simmer mixture. Sauté garlic in oil in another Dutch oven or frying pan until golden; add meat and fry 10–15 minutes. Drain excess grease and add meat and garlic to beans. Simmer 1–2 hours or until everyone gets back to camp. (Note: If you have leftover chili, reheat it and serve with eggs, warmed tortillas, and salsa for breakfast the next morning.)

SERVES 5 TO 6

Classic Green Chili Stew

Brown pork in oil in 12-inch Dutch oven over low heat on the stove or using about 12 briquets under the Dutch. Add onion and garlic as meat browns; cook about 5 minutes. While meat is browning, boil potatoes 5–10 minutes in Dutch oven or separate pot. Let cool, then cube. Add tomatoes, chilies, oregano, basil, and water. Simmer, covered, about 1 hour or until meat is fork tender. If necessary, add more water 1/2 cup at a time. Add potatoes and simmer about 30 minutes.

2 pounds pork, cubed
1 to 2 tbsps oil
2 medium onions, chopped
3 to 4 cloves garlic, minced
3 medium potatoes
2 10-oz. cans diced tomatoes
8 green chilies, coarsely chopped
1 tsp fresh oregano, chopped
1 tsp fresh basil, chopped
2 cups water or more as needed

SERVES 6

Variations:
If fresh oregano, basil, and chilies are not available, substitute dried equivalents for herbs and canned equivalent for chilies. If canned tomatoes contain basil, garlic, or oregano, omit those ingredients from recipe.

Baked Macaroni 'n' Cheese

OOOOOH!

1 10 3/4-oz. can cream
   of mushroom soup
1/2 cup milk
1/2 tsp mustard
1/4 tsp pepper
3 cups elbow macaroni,
   cooked
2 cups cheddar cheese,
   grated, divided
1 cup french fried onions

In 1 1/2-quart casserole, blend soup, milk, mustard, and pepper. Stir in macaroni and 1 1/2 cups cheese. Cover and bake at 400 degrees 25 minutes or until hot. Stir; then top with onions and remaining 1/2 cup cheese. Bake 5 minutes or until cheese melts.

SERVES 6

88

Sauerkraut Soup

1 cup sauerkraut
1 cup potatoes, cubed
5 cups water
1 cup sour cream
2 tbsps butter
3 tbsps flour
1 egg yolk
salt and pepper, to taste

Boil sauerkraut and potatoes in water 15 minutes. Mix together sour cream, butter, flour, and egg yolk; slowly add to soup mixture, stirring constantly. Heat thoroughly until well blended. Season to taste and serve. Great with rye bread.

SERVES 6

2 19-oz. cans cream of chicken soup
1 small onion, chopped
1 small jar (2 oz.) diced pimentos
4 medium potatoes, peeled and
    cut into 3/4- to 1-inch cubes
2 3 1/2-oz. cans precut chicken,
    mixed or breast
1 15-oz. can cream-style corn
1 15-oz. can whole kernel corn
2 cups milk
1 tsp pepper
1/4 tsp salt
1/4 tsp celery salt
other seasonings, if desired
Longhorn cheddar cheese, grated

Chicken Corn Chowder

Put all ingredients except cheese into large pan or Dutch oven. Cook until potatoes are cooked through and tender. Serve with cheese on top, about 15 to 20 minutes.

SERVES 8 TO 10

Chicken and Rice Soup

oil chicken breasts in stock until done, about 25–30 minutes. Remove breasts, reserving stock; cut into 1/2- to 1-inch cubes. Return chicken to stock. Bring to boil and reduce heat to simmer. Add onion, celery, rice, salt, and pepper. Simmer about 1 hour. Serve with hard toasted bread or crackers.

SERVES 8 TO 10

4 boneless skinless
  chicken breasts
4 cups chicken stock
1/2 cup onion, diced
1 celery heart (about 4
  small stalks), chopped

1 cup long grain rice,
  uncooked
1/2 tsp salt
1 tsp pepper

Twice-Baked Potatoes

10 medium russet baking potatoes
1/2 cup vegetable oil
2 sticks butter
3/4 cup onion, chopped
1 cup half and half
2 tsps salt
1/4 tsp pepper
1 cup cheddar cheese,
   shredded
chives (optional)

Wash and dry potatoes. Wipe with oil, lay on oven rack; bake at 375 degrees about 50 minutes. Remove from oven; cool. Melt butter and sauté onion. Cut each potato lengthwise and scoop out centers. Mash removed pulp in bowl with half and half. Mix in onion, salt, and pepper. Fill potato shells with mixture and top with cheese before baking. Garnish with chives, if desired. Bake 15 minutes at 350 degrees.

MAKES 20

Red Beans and Rice

2 cups dried red kidney beans
5 cups water, plus additional if needed
1 large onion, chopped
2 ribs celery, chopped
4 cloves garlic, chopped
salt and pepper, to taste
2 bay leaves
1 pound Polish sausage, cut into 1-inch cubes

SERVES 6 TO 8

Wash beans and soak overnight in cold water. When ready to cook, drain soaking water and place beans in large soup pot. Add water and bring to boil. Reduce heat until beans are just simmering. Add onion, garlic, celery, salt, pepper, and bay leaves. Add sausage; simmer 2 hours. If mixture is too dry, add more water. Serve over white rice or with cornbread.

93

Oven-Roasted Potatoes

4 to 6 medium
  potatoes, peeled
1 stick butter
salt
pepper
paprika

Boil potatoes about 15 minutes. Drain well and return to low heat 2 minutes to slightly dry them. Cut into wedges; put in buttered 2-quart casserole and top with pats of butter. About 1 hour before serving, put casserole in 375–400 degree oven. When butter has melted, turn potatoes; sprinkle salt, pepper, and paprika over potatoes. Repeat process every 10–15 minutes. Potatoes should be crisp and golden.

SERVES 8 TO 10

Sport
SUBURBAN

4 cups water
3 cups potatoes, peeled
   and diced
1 carrot, grated
1 onion, finely chopped
1 head fresh broccoli,
   chopped into bite-size
   pieces (optional)
1/4 cup butter
1/4 cup flour
2 cups milk
12 oz. Velveeta cheese,
   cut into chunks
salt and pepper
1 clove garlic, mashed

In large saucepan combine water, potatoes, carrot, onion, and broccoli, if desired. Boil until just tender. Drain, reserving water. In bottom of double boiler, boil water. In top of double boiler, combine butter and flour; stir to make paste. Add milk and cook, stirring constantly, until thickened and smooth. Add cheese a few chunks at a time to milk mixture. When thickened and all cheese is melted, add to potato mixture and blend well. Add salt, pepper, and garlic to taste.

Cheese and Potato Soup

SERVES 6 TO 8

Vegetable Soup

2 cups potatoes, cubed
3 cups tomato juice
1 cup cabbage, chopped
3/4 cup green beans, cut
   in 1-inch pieces
3/4 cup celery, diced
1 medium tomato, coarsely diced
1/2 cup carrots, sliced
2 parsnips, pared and diced
1 small onion, chopped
1 chicken or beef bouillon cube
salt, pepper, other seasonings, to taste

C ombine all ingredients in kettle or small stockpot and simmer uncovered 1–2 hours or until vegetables are tender. Add water if broth becomes too thick.

SERVES 6 TO 8

Mushroom and Barley Soup

2 tbsps butter or margarine
1/2 pound fresh mushrooms
1/2 cup onion, diced
1/2 cup celery, diced
1/2 cup carrot, diced

1 tbsp flour
3 cups chicken or
   beef broth
1/2 cup pearled
   medium barley

1 1/2 cups cooked
   chicken or beef, diced
salt, pepper, other
   seasonings, to taste
1 cup milk (optional)

I n 3-quart saucepan or Dutch oven melt butter; add mushrooms, onion, celery, and carrot. Cook over moderately low heat about 10 minutes, stirring often. Stir in flour, then broth. Add barley; cover and simmer until barley is cooked through, about 1 hour. Add meat and seasonings. For a cream soup, stir in milk. Reheat and serve in soup bowls.

SERVES 4

Country-Style Vegetable Beef Soup

4 quarts water
1 1/2 pounds ground
 or chopped beef or
 stew meat
12 black peppercorns
 (optional)
2 onions, chopped
1 16-oz. can tomatoes,
 cut up
1 15-oz. can tomato sauce
2 cups potatoes, diced

2 carrots, sliced
2 ribs celery, sliced
1 10-oz. package frozen
 green beans
1 10-oz. package frozen
 baby lima beans
1 10-oz. package
 frozen corn
salt and pepper, to taste
1 cup egg noodles
1 cup elbow or shell
 macaroni

In large covered pot, simmer water with beef and peppercorns, if desired, 1 1/2 hours. Remove from heat. Skim. Remove peppercorns. Add onions, tomatoes, and tomato sauce; bring to boil. Reduce heat and cook 1 hour. Add potatoes, carrots, celery, beans, and corn; cook 45 minutes. Add salt and pepper to taste. Add noodles and macaroni; cook until the noodles are done. If desired, thin with V-8 juice, water, broth, or tomato juice. (Note: Fresh vegetables may be used in place of frozen.)

SERVES 8 TO 12

Sauerkraut Salad

Dissolve vinegar and sugar. Bring to boil and cool. Pour over sauerkraut. Mix celery, onion, and pepper into sauerkraut. Refrigerate at least 24 hours. Serve with barbequed brisket for a great color and taste combination.

1/2 cup vinegar
2 cups sugar
2 15-oz. cans or pkgs
   sauerkraut, drained;
     if using canned, rinse
     in colander
1 cup celery, chopped
1 cup onion, chopped
1 green pepper, chopped

SERVES 8 TO 10

Jellied Cranberry Salad

1 pkg raspberry gelatin
1 cup hot water
1/2 cup cold water
1 small orange, peeled
  and diced
1/2 cup canned crushed
  pineapple, drained

1 16-oz. can whole
  cranberry sauce
1/3 cup nuts, chopped
sour cream or mayonnaise
crisp lettuce leaves

Dissolve gelatin in hot water. Add cold water and chill until partially thickened. Fold orange, pineapple, cranberry sauce, and nuts into gelatin. Pour into one large mold or individual molds and chill until firm. Turn out on chilled plate and serve with dollops of sour cream or mayonnaise, and garnish with lettuce leaves.

SERVES 6 TO 8

Marinated Five Bean Salad

1 15-oz. can kidney beans, drained
1 15-oz. can wax beans, drained
1 15-oz. can green beans, drained
1 15-oz. can garbanzo beans, drained
1 15-oz. can black-eyed peas,
    drained (optional)
1 15-oz. can peas, drained (optional)
1 medium onion, sliced
1 green pepper, sliced into rings
1/2 cup sugar
1/2 cup vinegar
1/2 cup salad oil
1 tsp salt
1/2 tsp dry mustard
1/2 tsp dried tarragon, crushed
2 tbsps parsley

Put beans, peas, onion, and green pepper in bowl. In separate bowl mix remaining ingredients until well blended. Pour over beans and vegetables. Chill several hours or overnight.

Tomato Shrimp Gelatin Salad

1 pkg lemon gelatin
1 cup boiling water
salt, to taste
1 cup cream of tomato soup
1/2 cup walnuts
1/2 cup sliced celery
1/2 cup chopped sweet pickles
1 6-oz. can shrimp, drained
1 1/2 tsps chili sauce
lettuce leaves
mayonnaise

Mix gelatin, water, and salt until dissolved. Add tomato soup and stir well. Add walnuts, celery, and pickles. Mix well and add shrimp and chili sauce. Chill until set. Serve on lettuce leaves with a dab of mayonnaise on top.

Asparagus with Lemon Sauce

1/4 cup butter
1/4 cup flour
2 cups milk

2 egg yolks, beaten
2 tbsps lemon juice
1 tsp salt

1/4 tsp pepper
2 pounds asparagus, cooked
toast

SERVES 8

Melt butter in pan over low to medium heat. Add flour a little at a time, mixing continuously to avoid forming lumps. Add milk gradually and continue mixing. Then add egg yolks, lemon juice, salt, and pepper, stirring well. Heat entire mixture to low boiling point. Arrange asparagus on toast and pour sauce over.

SERVES 8

3 tbsps butter or margarine
3 tbsps flour
1 1/2 cups milk
3/4 tsp salt
paprika, as desired
1/4 tsp Worcestershire sauce
2 cups American cheese, grated
1 medium cabbage, cut into
   6 to 8 wedges
8 thin slices precooked ham

Cabbage and Ham with Cheese Sauce

Melt butter or margarine in pan over low to medium heat. Add flour a little at a time, mixing continuously to avoid forming lumps. Add milk gradually and continue mixing. Add salt, paprika, and Worcestershire sauce. Stir in cheese and remove from heat as soon as cheese melts. In separate saucepan boil cabbage 8–10 minutes. Quickly pan fry ham slices while cabbage is boiling. Arrange ham slices and cabbage wedges on platter. Drizzle cheese sauce over both; serve immediately.

Scalloped Potatoes

1 can cream of celery soup
1/2 cup milk
1 small onion, chopped
salt and pepper, to taste
4 cups potatoes, peeled and sliced, divided

*P*reheat oven to 350 degrees. Combine soup, milk, and onion. Add salt and pepper to taste. In lightly oiled 9 x 9-inch baking dish, arrange 2 cups potatoes in layer. Pour half soup mixture over potatoes; add remaining 2 cups potatoes; pour remaining soup mixture over potatoes. Bake uncovered 1 hour or until potatoes are tender.

SERVES

Baked Acorn Squash

1 medium
  acorn squash
1 medium apple,
  cored and diced

1/4 cup raisins
3 tbsps honey
cinnamon

*P*reheat oven to 350 degrees. Cut squash in half lengthwise. Bake 20 minutes. Remove seeds. In bowl mix apples, raisins, and honey; spoon into each squash half; sprinkle with cinnamon. Bake 30 minutes in covered pan with about 1/4-inch water in bottom of pan.

DESSERTS

*H*istory doesn't make it clear who coined the phrase "sweet tooth," but I bet it had something to do with a cowboy on an 1850s trail drive. To him the phrase "long in the tooth" referred to a horse older than eight years because horses show their age — up to eight years — by the size of their teeth. Is it a stretch to imagine that if he craved sweets other cowpokes said he had a "sweet tooth"?

Today we consider dessert to be a common treat that culminates an evening meal, but it wasn't always so. On those long-ago trail drives to northern railheads, cowboys subsisted for weeks on the three Bs: beef, beans, and

WORTH A DRAW

biscuits. The cookie provisioned his chuck wagon with dried beans and as much flour as space and weight allowed. Though also considered staples, sweeteners such as sugar and molasses were used sparingly to make sure there was enough for the entire trip.

As the cowboys slowly trailed the herd across what seemed to be endless oceans of prairie, when they sighted a tree line in the distance, they quickened their pace. The tree line meant a stream, and prairie streams usually meant good water for the herd, a chance for a bath, and possibly wild fruit trees and berries. Desperate for something sweet, any cowpoke (especially one with a sweet tooth) wanting to improve his status with the cook made sure his saddlebags were bulging with fruit when he rode back to camp. At the home ranch, most self-respecting cowboys wouldn't think of picking fruit; but on the open range sitting on horseback made the picking easy! More than one old cookie endeared himself to the crew with a Dutch oven cobbler made with wild plums rustled up by that one sweet tooth cowboy.

As civilization worked its way west, homesteaders and ranchers alike quickly put in gardens and orchards. Today those hardy orchards are marked by only scraggly fruit trees and a couple of hills of rhubarb, though they provided desserts for generations of cowboys who were just as hardy.

Amy Tanner's Apple Crunch

6 Granny Smith
or Northern Spies
apples, sliced,
peeled (optional)

1/2 cup (2 bottles)
red cinnamon candies
1/4 tsp mace (optional)
1 tsp vanilla
crunch topping

*P*lace apples in 10-inch Dutch oven, distributing evenly. Sprinkle cinnamon candies evenly over apples. Sprinkle mace, if desired, and vanilla evenly over surface. Top with crunch mixture, distributing evenly over surface to form flat, even covering. Cover with lid. Bake 45–50 minutes with about 7 briquets under oven and about 16 on lid, or at 375 degrees. When done, topping should be starting to brown. Serve hot with the most decadent vanilla ice cream you can find.

Crunch:

3/4 cup sugar
1 cup flour
1/4 tsp mace

1/4 tsp salt
1/3 cup butter,
softened

Mix sugar, flour, mace, and salt in bowl. Cut in butter using pastry cutter. Mix until crumbly. Set aside.

Lazy Daisy Cake

2 eggs
1 cup sugar
1 tsp vanilla

1 cup cake flour
1 tsp baking powder
1/4 tsp salt

1/2 cup milk
2 tbsp butter
frosting

Combine eggs, sugar, and vanilla; beat until thick. Sift flour, baking powder, and salt; add to egg mixture. Heat milk and butter to boiling; add to mixture. Bake in buttered 8 x 8-inch pan at 350 degrees 30–40 minutes. Remove from oven, frost, and return to hot oven or broiler to brown.

SERVES 9

Icing:

3/4 cup brown sugar
1/2 cup butter, melted
1/4 cup cream
1 cup coconut

Combine all ingredients in small bowl and blend well. Frost as instructed.

Baked Custard

3 eggs, slightly beaten
1/3 cup sugar
dash salt
1 tsp vanilla
2 1/2 cups milk, scalded
ground nutmeg
very hot water

*P*reheat oven to 350 degrees. Mix eggs, sugar, salt, and vanilla. Stir in milk gradually. Pour into 6 6-ounce custard cups; sprinkle with nutmeg. Place cups in 13 x 9 x 2-inch pan; place in oven. Pour water into pan to within 1/2 inch of tops of cups. Bake until knife inserted halfway between center and edge of custard comes out clean, about 45 minutes. Remove cups from water. Serve warm or chilled.

SERVES 6

Caramel custard:

Before preparing custard, heat 1/2 cup sugar in heavy 1-quart saucepan over low heat, stirring constantly, until sugar is melted and golden brown. Divide syrup among custard cups; tilt cups to coat bottoms. Allow syrup to harden in cups about 10 minutes. Pour custard mixture over syrup; bake. Unmold and serve warm or, if desired, refrigerate and unmold at serving time. Caramel syrup will run down sides of custard, forming sauce.

Marshmallow custard:

Follow baked custard recipe. Place 1/4 cup miniature marshmallows in each cup before pouring in custard.

Ginger Snaps

3/4 cup shortening
1 1/2 cups sugar, divided
1 egg
1/4 cup molasses

2 cups sifted flour
1 1/2 tsps baking soda
1 tsp ground cloves
1 tsp ground cinnamon
1 tsp ground ginger

Cream together shortening and 1 cup sugar. Add egg and molasses; beat until smooth. Add flour, baking soda, cloves, cinnamon, and ginger. Beat until smooth. Make into teaspoon-size balls and roll in remaining 1/2 cup sugar. Bake on ungreased cookie sheet at 350 degrees 8–10 minutes.

MAKES 3 TO 6 DOZEN

Baked Rice Pudding

SERVES 6 TO 8

1/2 cup regular rice, uncooked
1 cup water
1 cup sugar, divided
1 tbsp cornstarch
dash salt

2 eggs, separated
2 1/2 cups milk
1 tbsp lemon juice
1/2 cup raisins
very hot water
ground cinnamon or nutmeg

Mix rice and water in saucepan. Heat to boiling, stirring once or twice. Reduce heat, cover, and simmer 14 minutes without removing cover. All water should be absorbed. Preheat oven to 350 degrees. Mix 1/2 cup sugar, cornstarch, and salt. Beat egg yolks slightly; beat yolks and milk into sugar mixture with hand beater. Stir in rice, lemon juice, and raisins. Pour into ungreased 1/2-quart casserole. Place casserole in 9 x 9 x 2-inch pan on oven rack; pour water into pan to 1 inch deep. Bake, stirring occasionally, until pudding is creamy and most liquid is absorbed, about 1 1/2 hours. Remove casserole from oven but not from pan of water. Increase oven temperature to 400 degrees. Beat egg whites on medium speed until foamy. Beat in 1/2 cup sugar on high speed, 1 tablespoon at a time; continue beating until stiff and glossy. Do not underbeat. Spread over pudding. Bake until meringue is golden brown, 8–10 minutes. Just before serving, sprinkle pudding with cinnamon or nutmeg. Serve warm. (Note: Omit meringue if desired.)

Bread Pudding

2 cups dry bread
2 cups milk, or enough
  to cover bread
2 eggs
1/2 cup sugar
1/4 tsp salt
1 tsp vanilla

Chocolate bread pudding:

Melt 2 tablespoons chocolate over hot water and add to soaked bread and milk, or put cocoa in soaked bread.

Raisin bread pudding:

Add 1/2 cup raisins with sugar, salt, and vanilla. Follow baking instructions and serve.

Soak bread in milk until very soft; mash until fine. Heat until nearly boiling. Beat eggs until light colored. Add sugar, salt, and vanilla. When mixed well, stir into bread mixture. Pour into 9 x 9-inch earthenware baking dish set in pan of water; bake at about 275 degrees 45 minutes.

SERVES 9 TO 12

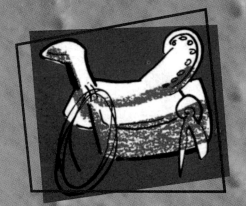

Graham Cracker Cake

1/2 cup butter, room temperature
1 cup sugar
3/4 cup milk
1 1/2 tsps baking powder
2 cups (about 26 single) graham
     crackers, crushed
1 tsp vanilla
1/2 cup walnuts, chopped
2 eggs

Cream butter and sugar until well blended. Add remaining ingredients one at a time and stir well after each addition. Pour into 8-inch square pan and bake at 375 degrees 45 minutes. Serve warm with whipped cream.

SERVES 6 TO 8

Oatmeal Chocolate Chip Cookies

1 cup sugar
1 cup brown sugar
1 cup butter or shortening
2 eggs
2 cups flour
1 tsp baking powder
1 tsp baking soda
1 tsp salt
1 tsp vanilla
2 cups oatmeal, uncooked
1 12-oz. pkg chocolate chips

Cream together sugar, brown sugar, and butter. Add eggs, flour, baking powder, baking soda, salt, and vanilla. Stir in oatmeal and chocolate chips. Drop by teaspoonfuls 2 inches apart on ungreased cookie sheet. Bake at 375 degrees 9–11 minutes.

MAKES ABOUT 5 DOZEN

Dutch Oven Apple Cake

1 cup vegetable oil
2 eggs
2 cups sugar
2 1/2 cups flour
1 tsp salt
1 tsp baking soda
2 tsps baking powder
1 tsp vanilla
3 cups apples, peeled
  and chopped
1 cup pecans, chopped

Mix oil, eggs, and sugar and beat until creamy. Sift dry ingredients together and add to egg mixture. Add vanilla, apples, and pecans. Mix well. Bake 45–50 minutes in lightly oiled 12-inch Dutch oven with 5–7 briquets underneath and 22–24 on lid.

SERVES 10 TO 12

118

2 cups flour
2 cups sugar
1 cup butter
3 tbsp cocoa
1 cup Coca-Cola
1 tsp baking soda

1/2 cup buttermilk
2 eggs, beaten
1 tsp vanilla
2 cups miniature
   marshmallows
icing

SERVES 8

Coca-Cola Cake

Preheat oven to 350 degrees. Combine flour and sugar in bowl. Melt butter in saucepan; add cocoa and Coca-Cola. Heat until just boiling. Cool slightly. Pour over flour mixture. Stir until blended. Dissolve baking soda in buttermilk; gradually add to flour mixture with eggs and vanilla. Mix well. Stir in marshmallows and pour into greased and floured 9 x 13-inch pan. Batter will be thin and marshmallows will come to top. Bake 35–40 minutes. Ice while cake is hot.

Icing:

1/2 cup butter
3 tbsps cocoa
6 tbsps
  Coca-Cola

1 pound
  confectioner's sugar
1 tsp vanilla
1 cup nuts, chopped

Combine butter, cocoa, and Coca-Cola in saucepan. Heat until boiling. Put sugar in electric mixer bowl and pour butter mixture over sugar. Beat until smooth. Add vanilla. Stir in nuts and set aside.

Sour Cream Pound Cake

1 cup butter-flavored
   shortening
3 cups sugar
6 eggs
1 cup sour cream
3 cups flour
1/4 tsp. baking soda
1/4 tsp. salt
2 tsp. vanilla or
   coconut flavoring

SERVES 8 TO 10

Preheat oven to 325 degrees. In mixing bowl cream shortening and sugar thoroughly. Add eggs, beating after each one. Add remaining ingredients a little at a time, beating thoroughly after each addition, until all are added. Pour batter into greased and floured 10-inch tube pan. Bake about 1 hour. Cool on wire rack. Remove from pan.

Rhubarb Cream Pie

3 cups rhubarb, diced
3 tbsp flour
2 eggs, separated
1 cup sweet cream
1 1/4 cups sugar

1/2 tsp vanilla
1/4 tsp cream of tartar
4 tbsps sugar
1 pie shell, unbaked

Mix rhubarb, flour, egg yolks, cream, and sugar.
Place in pie shell. Bake at 350 degrees 40 minutes.
Beat egg whites with vanilla and cream of tartar until
soft peaks form. Gradually add sugar, beating until stiff
and glossy peaks form. Spread meringue over hot filling.
Bake 12–15 minutes. Let cool, then refrigerate.
(Note: Best when thoroughly chilled.)

SERVES 8

Peach Cobbler

1 tbsp butter
6 large peaches, sliced
1 1/3 cups Bisquick-type
    baking mix
1/2 cup plus 1 tbsp
    sugar, divided
2/3 cup milk

1 tbsp oil
1 tsp ground cinnamon
1 tbsp cornstarch
1/2 cup boiling water
milk, ice cream, or
    whipped cream (optional)

Melt butter in bottom of 9-inch square pan. Put peaches over bottom. Mix together baking mix, 1 tablespoon sugar, milk, and oil. Spread evenly over peaches. Mix together remaining 1/2 cup sugar, cinnamon, and cornstarch. Sprinkle over dough, covering completely. Pour boiling water over top, completely moistening sugar mixture. Bake at 350 degrees 35–45 minutes. Serve warm with milk, ice cream, or whipped cream, if desired. (Note: For doubling recipe use 9 x 13-inch pan. Canned peaches can be used if drained thoroughly, using 2–3 21-oz. cans for 9-inch pan, 3–5 21-oz. cans for 9 x 13-inch pan.

SERVES 4 TO 6

Sweet Potato Pecan Pie

2 to 3 sweet potatoes for about 1 1/2
   cups cooked pulp (canned are okay)
1/2 cup light brown sugar, packed
3/4 cup plus 2 tbsps sugar, divided
1/2 egg, beaten until frothy
1 tbsp heavy cream
2 tbsps vanilla, divided
1/4 tsp ground cinnamon
1/4 tsp allspice

1/4 tsp ground nutmeg
1 cup light, dark, or
   blended corn syrup
2 eggs
1 1/2 tsps butter
dash cinnamon
1 cup pecan halves
1 cream cheese pie crust,
   unbaked, thoroughly chilled

If using fresh sweet potatoes, peel and cook in boiling water about 15 minutes or until tender. Cool and drain well before mashing. In large bowl combine sweet potatoes with brown sugar, 2 tablespoons sugar, 1/2 egg, cream, 1 tablespoon vanilla, cinnamon, allspice, and nutmeg; mix until smooth. Set aside. To make syrup, in another bowl stir together remaining 3/4 cup sugar, corn syrup, 2 eggs, butter, remaining 1 tablespoon vanilla, and cinnamon until mixture becomes slightly opaque, about 1 minute. Add pecans. Spoon sweet potato filling evenly into pie crust. Pour pecan syrup on top and bake at 325 degrees about 1–1 1/2 hours.

SERVES 8

Cream cheese pie crust:

6 oz. cream cheese
1/4 cup butter
2 cups flour
pinch salt

Allow cream cheese and butter to come to room temperature. Cut cream cheese and butter into flour and salt. Form soft dough into ball and chill. Roll well-chilled pastry dough to about 12-inch circle. Carefully place crust in deep pie pan and crimp edges. Fill crust according to directions above.

Frozen Lime Pie

2 eggs
1/2 cup sugar
1/2 cup light
   corn syrup
green food coloring
1 cup cream
1 cup milk

1/3 cup lime juice
1 tsp lime peel, grated
pinch salt
graham cracker pie crust,
   unbaked
strawberries or cherries
   for garnish

Beat eggs until lemon colored. Add sugar gradually until mixture is thick and custard like. Add remaining ingredients in order listed. Freeze with temperature control at coldest position or in deep freeze. When frozen remove to bowl and whip with beater until light and creamy. Fill chilled crust. Sprinkle remaining crust mixture and garnish with strawberries or cherries. Freeze until firm.

SERVES 8

Graham cracker pie crust:

20 graham crackers,
   rolled fine
1/2 cup powdered sugar
1/4 cup butter, melted

Blend crumbs with sugar and
butter. Line pie pan with 3/4
of crumb mixture and reserve
remaining 1/4. Set aside.

RECIPE INDEX

SIX-SHOOTER SOUPS & SIDES

DESSERTS WORTH A DRAW